University
for the
Creative Arts

Fort Pitt
Rochester
Kent
ME1 1DZ

Tel: 01634 888734
E-mail:
gatewayrochester@uca.ac.uk

*A BATHING APE®

APE SHALL
NEVER KILL APE

A BATHING APE
SINCE 1993

GATEFOLD LEGEND

PAGES 2 & 7:
INTERIOR VIEW OF
BAPE STORE® SHIBUYA
(2007), DESIGNED WITH
**MASAMICHI KATAYA-
MA/ WONDERWALL**

PAGES 3-6:
A BATHING APE® &
APEE® HOODIES
WITH CAMOUFLAGE
PATTERNS EXCLUSIVELY
CREATED FOR STORES,
TOP ROW (FROM LEFT
TO RIGHT) AOMORI,
AOYAMA, FUKUOKA,
HARAJUKU,HIROSHIMA,
HONG KONG, KAGO-
SHIMA,KANAZAWA,
OSAKA, & KYOTO

MIDDLE ROW (FROM
LEFT TO RIGHT)
LONDON, LOS ANGELES,
MAEBASHI, MATSUYAMA,
NAGOYA, NEW YORK,
NIIGATA, KUMAMOTO,
SAPPORO, SENDAI

BOTTOM ROW (FROM
LEFT TO RIGHT)
SHIZUOKA, TAIPEI,
YOKOHAMA, **APEE**®
HONG KONG, **APEE**®
OSAKA, **APEE**®
FUKUOKA, **APEE**®
MATSUYAMA, **APEE**®
SENDAI, **APEE**® NAGOYA,
APEE® TAIPEI

PAGE 8:
NIGO® IN HIS TOKYO
ATELIER, 2008

NIGO®
WITH AKIO IIDA AND IAN LUNA

ART DIRECTION BY AKIO IIDA
BOOK DESIGN BY IAN LUNA & LAUREN A. GOULD

GRAPHIC & EDITORIAL COORDINATION BY
YUKO TAKUMA, SHUHEI ODA & NAOKI SHIMAOKA

First published in the United States of America
by Rizzoli International Publications, Inc.
300 Park Avenue South, New York, NY 10010
www.rizzoliusa.com

Copyright Text © 2008
A Bathing Ape® / Nowhere Co., Ltd.,
NIGO®, Akio Iida and Ian Luna

Editors: Ian Luna & Lauren A. Gould
Editorial Consultant: Toby Feltwell
Project Manager: Yuko Takuma
Project Coordinator: Kana Kawanishi
Translation: Marie Iida, Lina Y. Hitomi
Editorial Assistants: Claire L. Gierczak,
Henry Casey & Moraiah Luna

Production: Maria Pia Gramaglia, Kaija Markoe,
Colin Hough Trapp & Walter de la Vega

Design Consultants: Chip Kidd & Mark Melnick
Production Consultant: Eugene Lee

All rights reserved. No part of this publication may
be reproduced, stored in a retrieval system, or
transmitted in any form or by any means, electronic,
mechanical, photocopying, recording, or otherwise,
without prior consent of the publishers.

2008 2009 2010 2011 / 10 9 8 7 6 5 4 3 2 1
Library of Congress Control Number: 2008933252
ISBN-13: 978-0-8478-3051-0
Printed in China

*A BATHING APE®

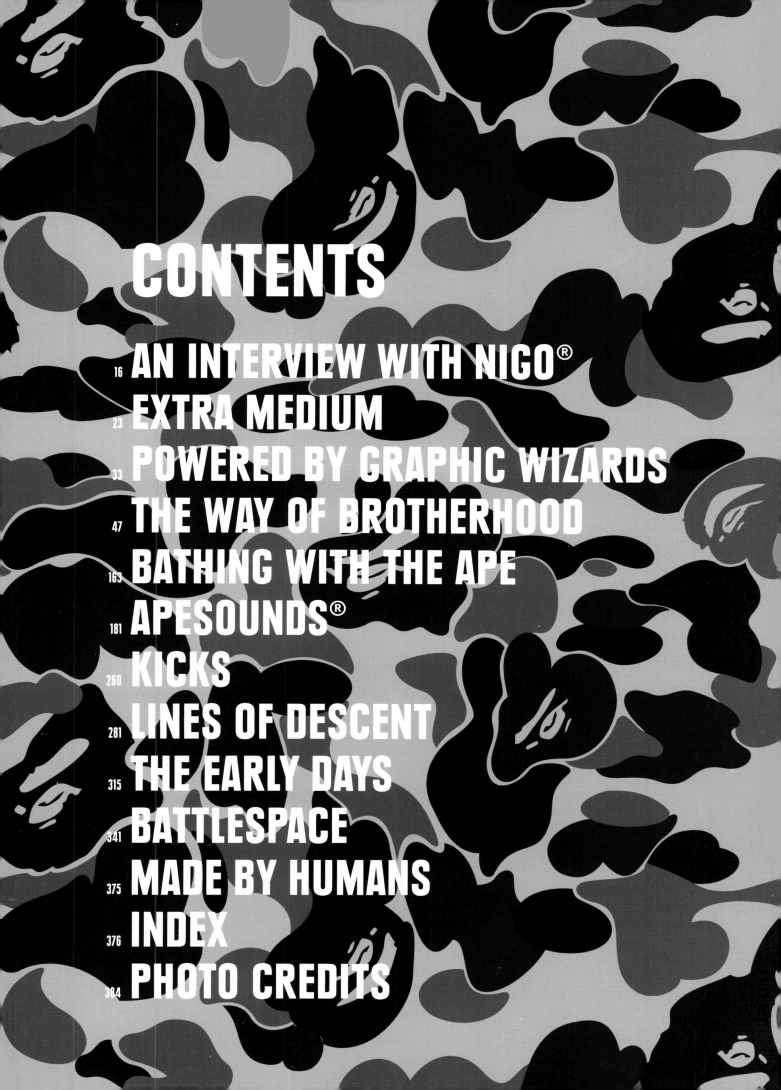

CONTENTS

A HIGHER PRIMATE:

It has been fifteen years since the birth of A BATHING APE® in the backstreets of Harajuku. In 1993, NIGO®—together with Jun Takahashi, aka JONIO, the designer of UNDERCOVER—took the first steps towards a defining career in fashion by opening a small, bare-bones shop. With no experience and almost as little to sell, could NIGO® have had any idea then of the outrageous following that the brand would generate? The intervening years have been a period of phenomenal transition and upheaval for BAPE®, its creator, and Harajuku itself—and a large chunk of that history is condensed in this book.

While it is almost inconceivable that Harajuku could foster such enterprising talent, given its present-day inertia, back then the neighborhood was at the height of its creative powers. In the grip of this ferment, a group of young creators gave rise to an entirely new, streetwise culture, one that only a truly postmodern condition could inspire and sustain. The bubble economy had burst, but the pioneers of Ura-Harajuku had a decidedly cynical view of a society that seemed unable to resuscitate itself from the shock. Armed with a DIY spirit and a mania for hand-made goods, their fashions forwarded a restatement of youth culture, an antidote to the mass-produced trends that dominated the scene in the early 1990s. In the process, they introduced a unique retailing model, built around a collaborative approach to design, that would reverberate beyond Tokyo and transform global fashion. Their initiatives became known as the Ura-Harajuku Movement, an authentic social phenomenon in Japan that crowned NIGO® and his contemporaries as cultural icons—a tightly knit group of twenty-somethings who breathed new life and conviction to the Japanese fashion industry. Not limited to apparel, their activities became a metric for gauging the pulse and direction of Tokyo's creative classes.

Throughout the 1990s, the progress of Macintosh design tools became the ideal weapons of the graphic wizards at A BATHING APE®—cult designers whose elusive existences only hinted at the creative depth of the brand. They gave rise to cutting-edge products that maximized the persuasive appeal of graphic design. Promoting the brand largely through word of mouth with no express advertising, but with the strategic assistance of key magazine editors, BAPE® became an irresistible streetwear phenomenon. Radiating from Tokyo, and fueled by the technological reach of the internet and mobile telephony, national borders were no longer relevant considerations to the brand's sphere of influence, and the longevity of the brand was assured because NIGO® did not fail to reach out to subsequent generations of consumers.

NIGO®: At its inception, NOWHERE was like a boutique store. It's hard to think about it now but I used to go on a buying spree for the shop once a month all by myself. I would send myself back an unbelievable amount of clothes I'd purchased abroad in separate Pelican Mail parcels, and then would have to pick them up at their branch in Setagaya once they arrived in Japan. Eventually, the whole routine became a bit tiresome and going to the States felt too much like a chore; I guess that became one of the catalysts for starting my own label. At the time, I had also started making t-shirts with JONIO as part of a series called "Last Orgy". Thanks to the influence of certain magazines they sold pretty well. I told JONIO that this was so much easier and that's when he said, " Why don't you do something on your own?"—the rest is history.

Akio Iida: SKATETHING, one of the supporting players who helped NIGO® build A BATHING APE®, reflected on this seminal period in their collective history: "Back then a lot of people in our immediate circle had already established clothing stores. Also, I believe both JONIO and NIGO® attained enormous popularity for the series they did in magazines," he said. "I think their generation had this united vigor and sense of aspiration. So when APE started it did not feel like anything too special; it just felt like the beginning of a new project." But in many ways, it signified the beginning of something entirely new, that had no precedent in Harajuku. Yet the movement arose not on the high street but in the back alleys.

N: The store gradually attracted more traffic, and as society's perception of us began to change, Harajuku itself underwent a rebirth. We moved offices quite a bit in Harajuku back then. It wouldn't be worth comparing it to what we have now,

AN INTERVIEW WITH NIGO®

but by the time we moved to an office near Takeshita-Guchi (the Takeshita Station exit of the JR Line) the structure of the company had already been established. SKATETHING and MANKEY, his classmate at Bunka Fashion College, would line up their desks side-by-side, and that was the exact point in time when we were solidly incorporated. I thought if we were going to do this right, we might as well do it like a proper outfit. But that didn't mean we had a distinctive brand concept yet. As long as the people closest to us were having a good time, I was happy. Back in those days everything was hand-screened. After ordering the raw t-shirts, we brought them over to the factory along with SKATETHING's design and explained the concept in person. A few days later we would bring back the finished products to Harajuku and distribute them to friends, and only then would we line them up at the storefront. That was so much fun and we couldn't get enough of it; everyone around us was just having a blast—we always had something going on every single day. For much of society, we were just a bunch of slacker kids, but yes, what we had done was unprecedented and unthinkable because we had managed to build our own store and identity from scratch and, changed Harajuku in the process.

Since SKATETHING was good friends with Cornelius (Keigo Oyamada), he was nice enough to wear a lot of Ape labels when we first started. At the time Cornelius was influential even in the major music scene as a proponent of *Shibuya-kei* (The Shibuya Sound), and our public image probably benefited from his contribution. In the midst of all that was happening around us, A BATHING APE® exploded as a major label and company.

I think I've always had a bit of an inferiority complex, but that negative energy fuels my rebellion and that was how I've always pushed myself forward. It has always been the source of power behind all my creativity and other endeavors. I still drive with that mentality. You know when fishermen talk wistfully about the "one that got away?" I want to be that fish.

I: It is clear that what NIGO® calls "negative energy" has always been a generative force for A BATHING APE®. Never one to stand front-and-center, his complexes may be the key to all that delightful eccentricity. But at the same time, he abhors being a follower. While some make light of the brand's achievements, the trajectory of A BATHING APE®'s ascent was always founded on hard work, persistence—and a fair amount of trial-and-error.

N: In the beginning, we weren't particularly significant in Japan and when we first started the shop in London, we were portrayed pretty ironically and even negatively. But all that changed when we launched in New York. There was this great "welcome to New York" -vibe from the onset and we got rave reviews from American media and the fans. When you get a critical nod from the States, the typical outcome is that Japanese automatically start to take notice. Over these fifteen years, the brand and the company have grown tremendously as we gained experience. In that process our ambitions became bigger and our ideas more controversial, and in order to make them into reality we realized we needed to take on the big corporations. The extent of what you can do is dependent on money, obviously, and in that sense it's true we have had a lot of ideas in the past we could not realize. Actually, there were offers to make the company public, but ultimately I decided that I could not sacrifice my position as a creator. All things considered, it basically came down to our responsibilities as creators that require us to be always one step ahead of the current trends. If we were to go public, we would need to deal with stockholders and other people that might not necessary share our aesthetic, and we would risk losing our edge. So, I turned that option down.

I've been saying for quite some time that Japanese designers do not have a lot of appeal. Ideally, we should be the type of people that are the most attractive and charismatic, but the current condition in Japan is far from it. Overseas, especially in European countries, there is a hallowed status for designers, but for designers based in Japan, their social recognition is still relatively low. Here, a designer's life and reputation is comparatively modest, and I wanted to revolutionize that.

We are about to set up shop in LA [editor's note: the store opened in April 2008], but as far as the balance of supply and demand goes, we are severely lacking in product. We don't necessarily feel compelled to remedy that. If the store's too bare we'd be inciting the growth of knock-offs and that's no good at all, but we don't want our concern for knock-offs and counterfeits to be the source of our motivation either.

I: This is clearly a problem inherent with anything that combines global aspirations with exclusivity. NIGO® is bent on seducing a much larger audience outside Japan and now sees the West as well as Asia as his field of battle and playground. Sadly, I do agree that Harajuku is in decline, no longer capable of keeping up with the speed and sensibilities of A BATHING APE®.

N: Yes, Harajuku today is no longer what it was, it's no longer provocative and I have no sentimental affection for it. Tokyo itself has lost a certain spark that existed in the past, and I think that young people's regard for fashion has depreciated. They now purchase clothes online with their mobile phones, so the meaning of going to the stores yourself and feeling the article of clothing in your hands has lost its relevance to many. Sure, Omotesando and Roppongi may look prettier, but all that are left are rows of high-end foreign labels and there is no passion there. What matters so much more to me these days is the fact that I challenged myself by opening a store in Shibuya, and it's actually been doing pretty well, with pretty solid reviews. As a result of the brand's popularity, and my attaining a more diverse and nuanced way of communicating to the public, I've become far more committed to my aesthetic as a designer. It's interesting because while some customers have an excellent sense of style, others are overtly APE from head-to-toe. So as a brand, I think it's important that I create what I want with a strong sense of identity as a designer. Our hoodies line has been a massive hit, and that brought on a deluge of imitations. I expected that to a certain degree, but that wasn't what I was hoping for either; I just feel like I can't stay at the same spot for too long and that propels me to keep creating new things.

Ultimately, I'm at a turning point right now and perhaps this book could serve as a form of closure, in a way. This is our 15th anniversary and it's imperative that we continue to evolve as a brand, to maintain our sights on the world, and in order to do so it will become necessary to rethink the playbook of how I've always done things. I'm sure there will be a lot of resistance to change but that's inevitable. That's just one of the drawbacks of the industry I'm in. To be honest, since I'm at a point again where I want to reconsider the identity of the brand, and seeing that I can no longer find inspiration in Tokyo, I don't consider Japan as an objective. From now on, I want to focus on Asia with Hong Kong as a launching pad. China's cultural growth is still at an early stage but it will be accelerated due to the internet, and I expect the situation to turn around dramatically. It would be fun if I could develop a kind of pan-Asian unity in the process.

On the other hand, a part of me is well aware that I'm visible because I'm from Tokyo. I frequently hear people say "when you go to Tokyo, you've got to first meet this cool dude named NIGO®." If you were to meet me in America, for instance, that would be unexceptional; it's significant because despite my misgivings, Tokyo still elicits a sense of wonder. Perhaps it means that the world has finally caught up to what we have been doing, or perhaps because the scale of what we can pull off has become so much bigger, and the fun in doing it more extreme. I still personally feel that the current Japanese music and fashion cultures are stagnant, and I hope that I can somehow contribute to a movement that compares to the astonishment I felt when I was young and first heard, lets say, Public Enemy or Run DMC. I want Tokyo to always be an exciting city, a society that everyone will still see as naughty and outlandish. It is out of that hope that I still attempt to communicate to the next generation what is culturally fundamental and important. For instance, I want to say that while everything is becoming rapidly digitized, an analog aesthetic is just as valuable. I don't quite mean for us to become a textbook example, but when young people look at what Ape is doing, I want them to consider our unique shops, our bizarre graphics, and remark that "here is a brand that's doing something interesting." I want them to look at what we are doing and sense that there are other paths to the future beyond the digital.

I do feel that I am a pioneer that broke out of Japan. What I've personally experienced is that it's possible to make any number of dreams a reality—and it all depends on your effort and drive. It sounds trite, but I want nothing more than for younger generations to draw sure strength from this ethic.
—April 2008, translated by Marie Iida

EXTRA MEDIUM

Just as Ralph Lauren is known for their polo shirts, the t-shirt is both a staple and a symbol of A BATHING APE®. It's expressive and uncomplicated at the same time, making it a medium best suited to our needs. —NIGO®

The history of A BATHING APE® began with the t-shirt.

NIGO® witnessed the rise and fall of the "Designer and Character boom," a *wasei-eigo* (Japanese English) shorthand for the explosion of high-fashion makes in 1980s, followed by the popularity of vintage clothing and the American casual or *Amekaji* look. His encounter with denim and chino shorts—the so-called "work wear" introduced by the latter trend— was instrumental to his opening NOWHERE, a shop he co-produced with JONIO (aka Jun Takahashi, the designer of UNDERCOVER).

Before he even had a brand, NIGO® would take solitary pilgrimages to America almost every month to accumulate vintage goods as well as a deeper knowledge of the trade as he maintained his shop in Ura-Harajuku. But the presence of JONIO and other streetwear pioneers within their immediate orbit who had already launched their own labels goaded NIGO® to switch gears and create a fashion identity he could call his own. The result was A BATHING APE®, and the brand's first contribution to the world was the graphic t-shirt.

At the time, the public perception of the t-shirt was a workaday article of clothing exiled to the farthest corner of the wardrobe. While a modest budget exercised limits on production, the inaugural line of t-shirts emblazoned with iron-on prints and designed by SKATETHING—a key NIGO® collaborator from the earliest days—had a distinctively handmade feel, and they soon lined the nondescript storefront, paired with another iconic item, the chino shorts.

NIGO®'s encyclopedic knowledge of *Amekaji* and the vintage trade contributed to his finely honed instinct, and in the D.I.Y. hothouse of Harajuku, a streetwear phenomenon was born. The persistent rumor was that a dinky store in one of the backstreets was selling t-shirts with a logo of a monkey's face, and that they were flying—nay swinging—off of the shelves. Word-of-mouth acquires near-digital speeds in Tokyo, and before long, the long lines of shoppers outside the store became a frequent sight.

The fortuitous combination of three factors contributed to the rise of the streetwear movement of the early 1990s: fashion magazines held unparalleled power and influence as a source of information for young people; Tokyo's club culture underwent a revival with the ascent of the DJ; and lastly, the place where all the movers and shakers convened became Harajuku. NIGO® and A BATHING APE® moved inexorably and undeniably to the center of this hive of competition and collaboration. As the brand acquired national and international recognition, the t-shirt remains the ultimate medium, and its importance to the brand is unchanged to this day.

PRECEEDING SPREAD: THE FIRST **NOWHERE STORE,** HARAJUKU, 1993

OPPOSITE PAGE: **BAPE**® T-SHIRT, 1993

FOLLOWING SPREAD: AN ASSORTMENT OF **BAPE**® T-SHIRTS

OPPOSITE PAGE:
LIMITED EDITION
T-SHIRT TO
COMMEMORATE
THE RELEASE
OF **JAY-Z'S THE
BLUEPRINT,**[2] 2002

THIS PAGE:
PATTERNED
LOGO FOR **N.E.R.D**
(NO ONE EVER
REALLY DIES),
FOUNDED BY
**PHARRELL WILLIAMS,
CHAD HUGO** & **SHAY
HALEY**

ABOVE:
VINYL FIGURES OF
THE BEASTIE BOYS,
1999

OPPOSITE PAGE:
THE BEASTIE BOYS X
BAPE®

POWERED BY GRAPHIC WIZARDS

BAPE® CAMO does what the monogram does for Louis Vuitton. It symbolizes A BATHING APE®—NIGO®

Basic items such as t-shirts, jeans, and hoodies constitute the core of A BATHING APE® as a brand, and the collection owes its seasonal transformation and mutation to the power of graphic design.

Acutely influenced by pop art, NIGO® saw the t-shirt as a natural medium for visual experiment, and a singular means of incorporating a strong graphic sensibility into fashion. The presence of two design prodigies—SKATETHING and MANKEY—was decisive in adding value to NIGO®'s ideas.

The brand's original camouflage pattern, known as BAPE® CAMO, is the most recognizable work born out of the collaboration between NIGO® and his principal graphic artists. The design was created in 1994 after NIGO® came up with blending the Apehead logo with a camouflage pattern he'd seen on a trip to the United States. Suggesting the concept to SKATETHING on his return, the new pattern was subsequently utilized in a number of products, eventually becoming synonymous with the brand's image and its material culture. Multiple color and design variations to the original olive pattern emerged annually for the next fifteen years. The library now boasts an impressive number of patterns, much expanded from the three basic colorways of olive, blue and pink; to sought-after exclusives NIGO® conceived with the Brooklyn-based KAWS.

These proprietary designs owe much of their graphic identity to disruptive patterns employed by branches of the US Armed Forces since the Second World War. The trademark scheme is itself directly adapted from the "frog skin" or "duckhunter" patterns used on reversible tropical uniforms and fabric helmet covers worn by the US Marines in the Pacific War. Migrating to decidedly non-military spec, BAPE® CAMO is now applied on everything from custom padded covers for the Eames Wire Chair to plastic file folders. Most notable are the unique patterns that have been employed to distinguish each of BAPE®'s thirty-odd retail locations to date, ranging in hue from the monochromatic greys of the Aoyama Bapexclusive store to the bright greens and yellows of the Hong Kong shop.

OPPOSITE PAGE:
F/W, 1996-1997

FOLLOWING SPREAD:
BIGGIE SMALLS, 1997;
CAMO PATTERN, 1995

PAGES 36-37:
BAPESTAR CAMO,
F/W 2001-2002 (L);
BEACH CHAIR FOR
CHISO GALLERY, KYOTO
(2001), DESIGNED WITH
**MASAMICHI KATAYAMA/
WONDERWALL** (R)

PRECEDING SPREAD:
NEON CAMO PATTERN,
S/S 2007 (L); **BAPE
STORE**ˢ **HONG KONG**,
2006 (R)

THIS PAGE: SHIRT, S/S
2008

OPPOSITE PAGE:
RESORT CAMOUFLAGE
PATTERN, S/S 2008

FOLLOWING SPREAD:
INTERIOR OF **BAPE
STORE**ˢ **HONG KONG**
(2006), DESIGNED WITH
**MASAMICHI KATAYA-
MA/ WONDERWALL**

OPPOSITE PAGE:
CAMO PATTERN
F/W 2005-2006

THIS PAGE:
YUKO HASHIMOTO
F/W 2005-2006

THE WAY OF BROTHERHOOD

I define collaboration as something I agree to do only with people I like. Generally, I do not accept outside proposals. When I do collaborate, everything must be strictly fifty-fifty—from creative stance to perspective.—NIGO®

While "collaboration" among distinct fashion brands is now a globally prevalent mode of production, its evolution gathered critical mass in the mid-1990s, and is linked inextricably to the unique, hothouse conditions that existed in Harajuku. During this key period, Harajuku-based brands coined the term "W(Double)-Name" for collaborative products and related initiatives. The creation of Double-Name goods, spearheaded by A BATHING APE® and other seminal labels, refined a unique market model that already operated under the draconian laws of the Limited Edition. With their supply forcibly rationed, the word-of-mouth appeal of these special releases incited a following that, not incidentally, also enhanced the value of already scarce regular production items. The notoriety of these premier goods led to long lines forming at the stores a full day before their release and their prices skyrocketed to unprecedented heights.

Initially, NIGO® as well as other grassroots designers and creators of Harajuku had simply set out to produce clothes that they and their close friends could wear. At the top rank of the Harajuku fashion avant-garde, these proprietor/designers had no reservations about making daily trips to one another's offices, paving the way for free-flowing, creative sessions that churned out products that mediated the strict divide between brand identities. Harajuku became the temporal hub of this production style, supported by a concept liberated from established fashion norms, and from there it captured the public imagination even as various corporations began to take notice.

The growing influence of the internet also paved the way for the international exposure of these joint experiments. For most established Western designers at the time, the idea of rivals in the same industry joining ranks to create products—or even entire product lines—was generally unheard of, and seen as absurd or self-defeating. This institutional resistance only focused worldwide interest in Tokyo streetwear, simultaneously driving up the appeal and influence of Harajuku brands. A BATHING APE®'s highly visible tie-ups with established global media—such as Disney, Nintendo and both Marvel and DC comics were borne out of the astonishing foresight and business savvy that NIGO® and his circle of friends had in no small measure.

NIGO® is also credited for expanding the collaborative possibilities of fashion and art well before other established luxury goods conglomerates bought into the concept wholesale, having been the first to work together with artists like FUTURA, STASH, KAWS, Gary Panter and Hajime Sorayama.

OPPOSITE PAGE:
BAPE® X **PEPSI COLA**
PROOF-OF-PURCHASE
STICKER, 2001

THIS PAGE:
BAPE® X **PEPSI COLA**
500ml BOTTLE, 2001

OPPOSITE PAGE:
PEPSI COLA
CAMPAIGN NOVELTY

FOLLOWING SPREAD:
BAPE® X **PEPSI COLA**
VENDING MACHINE,
2003; **NIGO®**, 2001

49

THIS PAGE:
BAPE® X **M·A·C**
THIRD EDITION 2005

OPPOSITE PAGE:
BAPE® CAMOUFLAGE
BODY PAINTING, 2004

THIS PAGE:
MARVEL X **BAPE STA**™
THE FANTASTIC FOUR,
F/W 2005-2006

OPPOSITE PAGE:
CLOCKWISE FROM
TOP LEFT, **MARVEL** X
BAPE STA™ F/W2005-
2006; THE X-MEN,
THE HULK, THE SILVER
SURFER, CAPTAIN
AMERICA, SPIDERMAN,
THOR & IRONMAN,
™ & © **MARVEL**

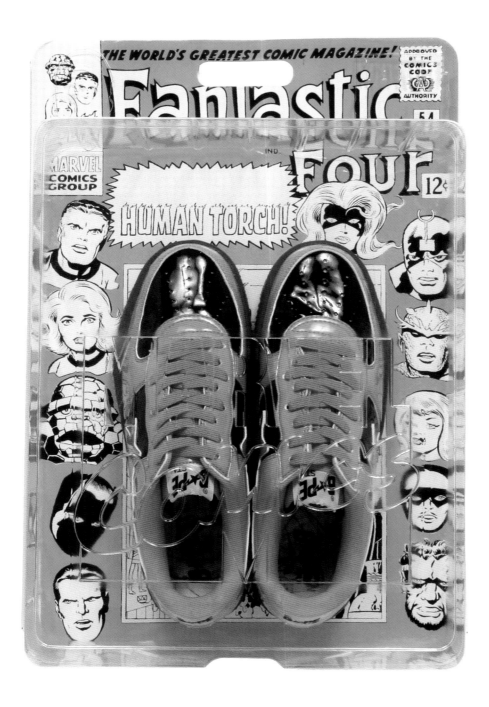

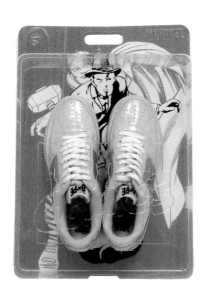

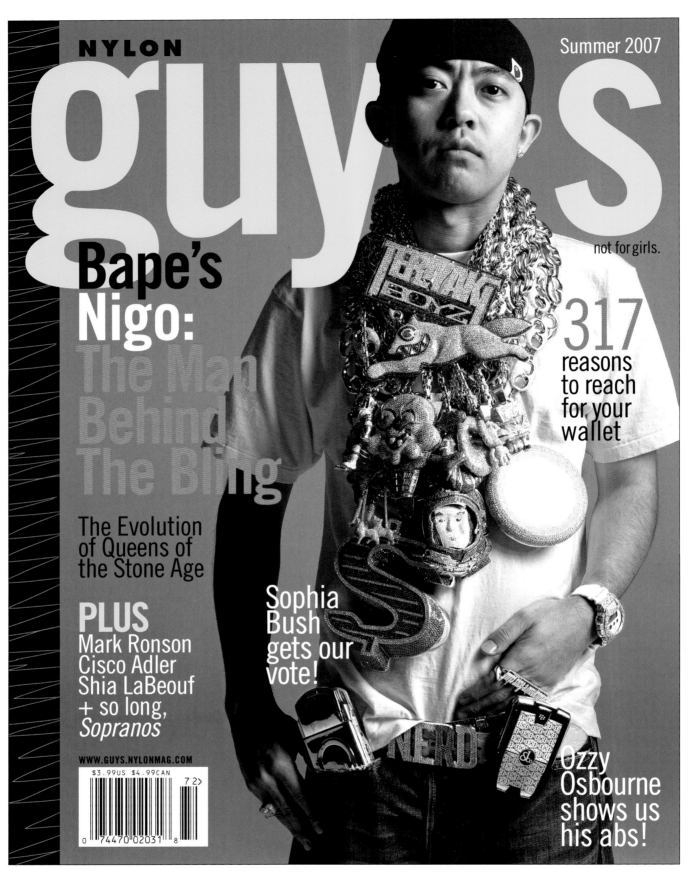

NYLON

guys

Summer 2007

not for girls.

Bape's Nigo:
The Man Behind The Bling

The Evolution
of Queens of
the Stone Age

PLUS
Mark Ronson
Cisco Adler
Shia LaBeouf
+ so long,
Sopranos

WWW.GUYS.NYLONMAG.COM

$3.99US $4.99CAN

72>

0 74470 02031 8

317
reasons
to reach
for your
wallet

Sophia
Bush
gets our
vote!

Ozzy
Osbourne
shows us
his abs!

ABOVE:
NIGO® ON THE COVER
OF *NYLON GUYS*,
SUMMER, 2007

OPPOSITE PAGE:
JACOB & CO.
CHRONOGRAPH

THIS SPREAD:
NAKATA.NET X **BAPE**®
SPECIAL ITEMS FOR
2006 WORLD CUP
IN GERMANY
© **NAKATA.NET**

**Sharing the Hopes and
Dreams in Germany, Together!**

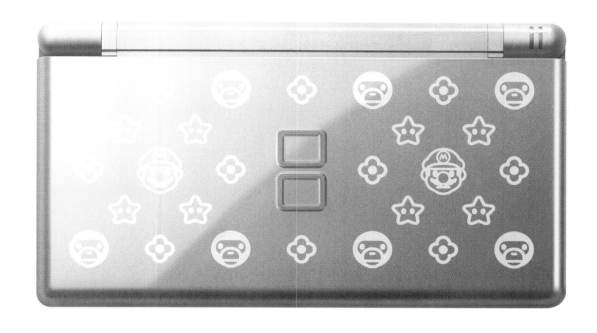

SEPTEMBER 2007 NO.132

萬麗 國際中文版

NIGO™
億萬少年的秘密
帶領 BAPE™ 軍團
從原宿進攻全世界

定價 NT$200

9 771028 003007

wanna be
Famous?

成名的條件你有沒有 > 成名的代價你要不要 > 名氣是否可以永續經營
如何從醜聞中全身而退 > 陶子 & 詹仁雄談人紅的道理

OPPOSITE PAGE:
DC X BAPE STA™,
BATMAN™ F/W 2007-
2008. ™ & © DC
COMICS. (s07)

THIS PAGE:
NIGO® ON THE COVER
OF *GQ TAIWAN*,
SEPTEMBER 2007

THIS PAGE:
BAPE X **HELLO KITTY**,
2005-2006

OPPOSITE PAGE:
BAPE X **HELLO KITTY**,
FOR *NUMERO
TOKYO*, 2008

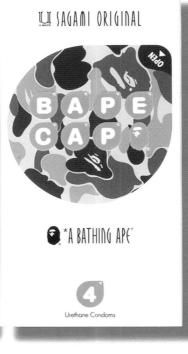

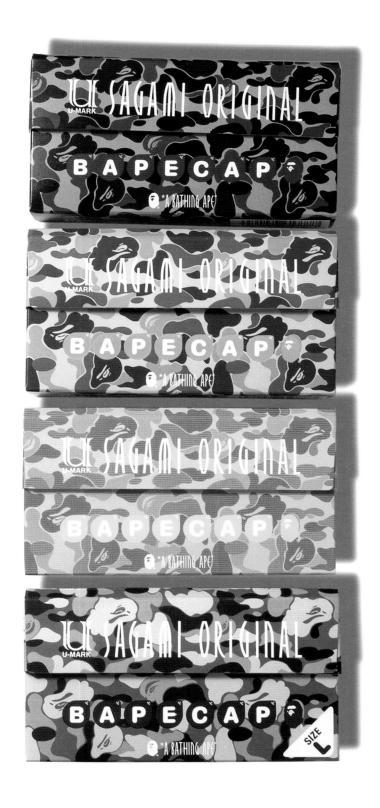

THIS PAGE:
BAPE® X **VERSACE**
FOR *VOGUE NIPPON*
CHARITY AUCTION,
2004

OPPOSITE PAGE:
BAPE® X **TATAMI®**
S/S 2007
© SHOEMASTER

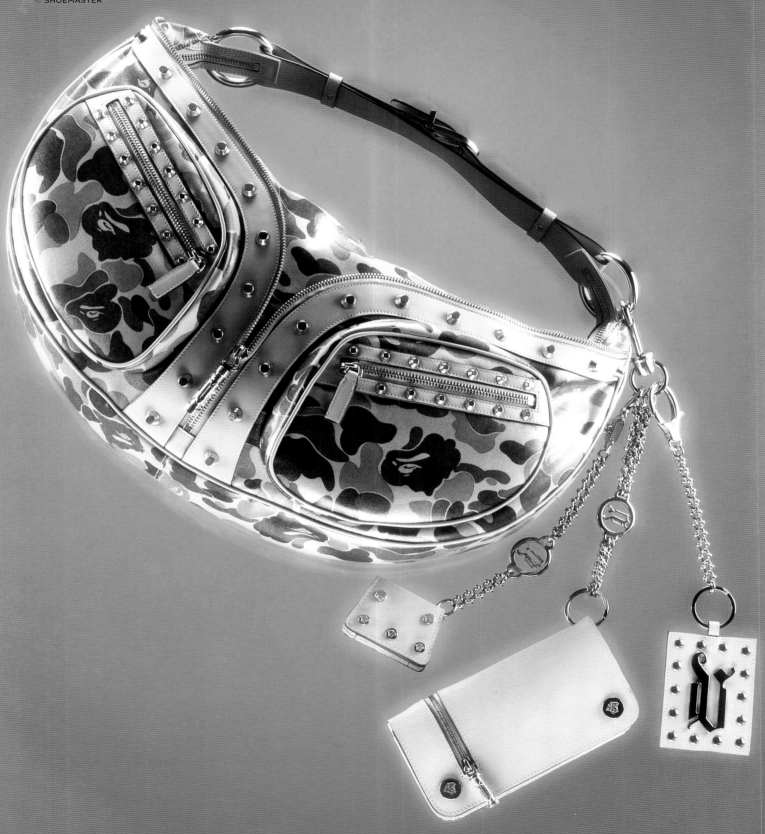

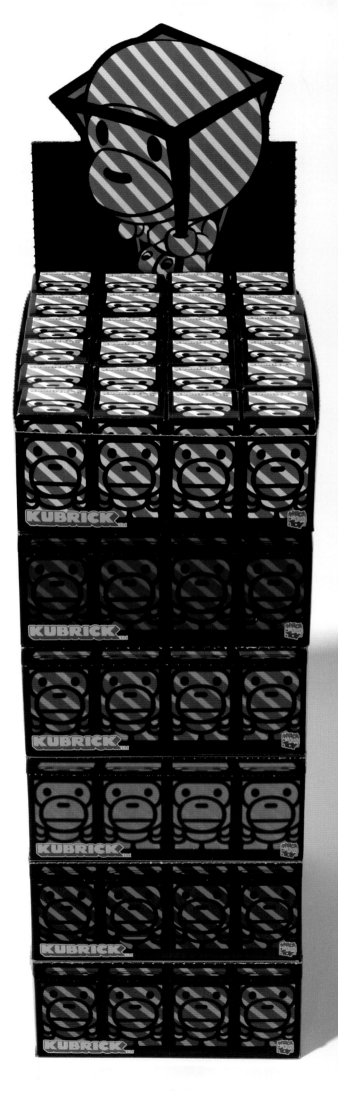

想いをつなぐ24時間。ことしで30回を迎えます。

24HOUR TELEVISION 30

24時間テレビ30「愛は地球を救う」
8月18日（土）夜6:3〇

●メインパーソナリティー／タッキー＆翼　●チャリティーパーソナリティー／黒木瞳　新庄剛志　●番組パーソナリティー／タカアンドトシ　●総合司会／徳光和夫　西尾由佳理（日本テレビアナ
●スペシャルドラマ／「君がくれた夏 ガンと闘った息子の730日」滝沢秀明　深田恭子 ほか　募金の方法や、募金の使われ方など、チャリティーに関する詳しい情報はホームページをご覧下さ

h24

年のテーマ『人生が変わる瞬間』
ー19日（日）夜 8:54
●チャリティーマラソンランナー／萩本欽一
時間テレビ公式HP www.ntv.co.jp/24h

8/18▶19　日テレ

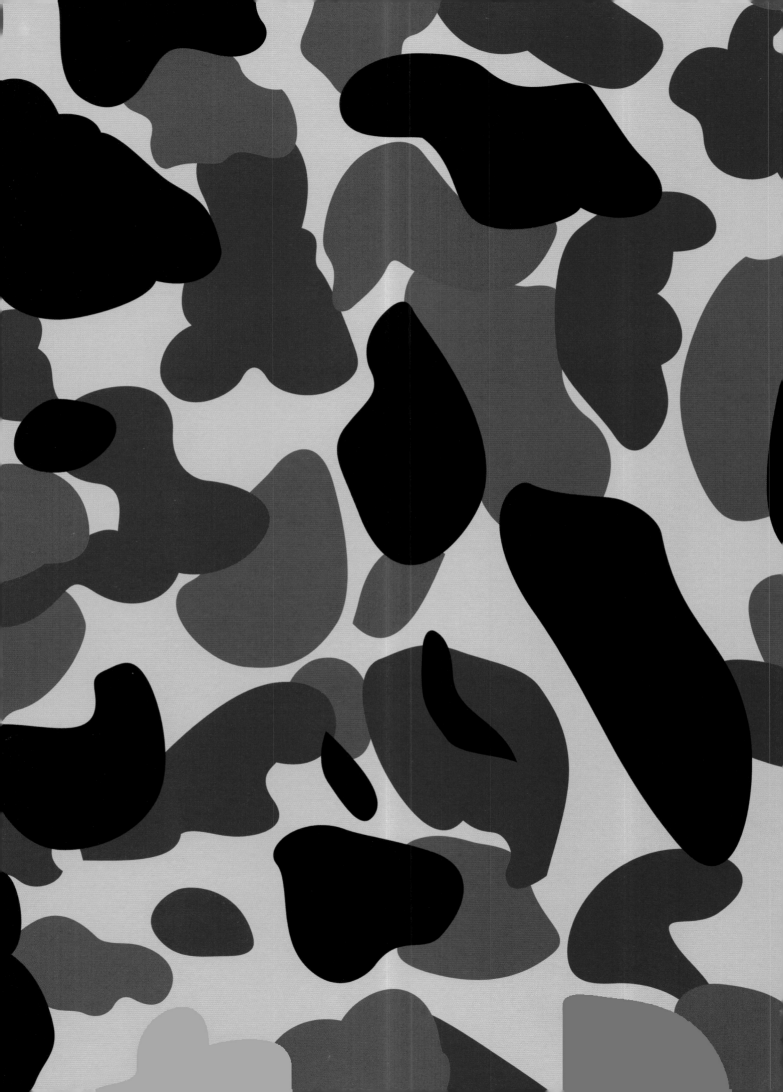

PRECEDING SPREAD:
BAPE® SAND CAMO
PATTERNS, 1997

THIS SPREAD:
JUMPSUIT AND CAMO
PATTERN, F/W 1997-1998

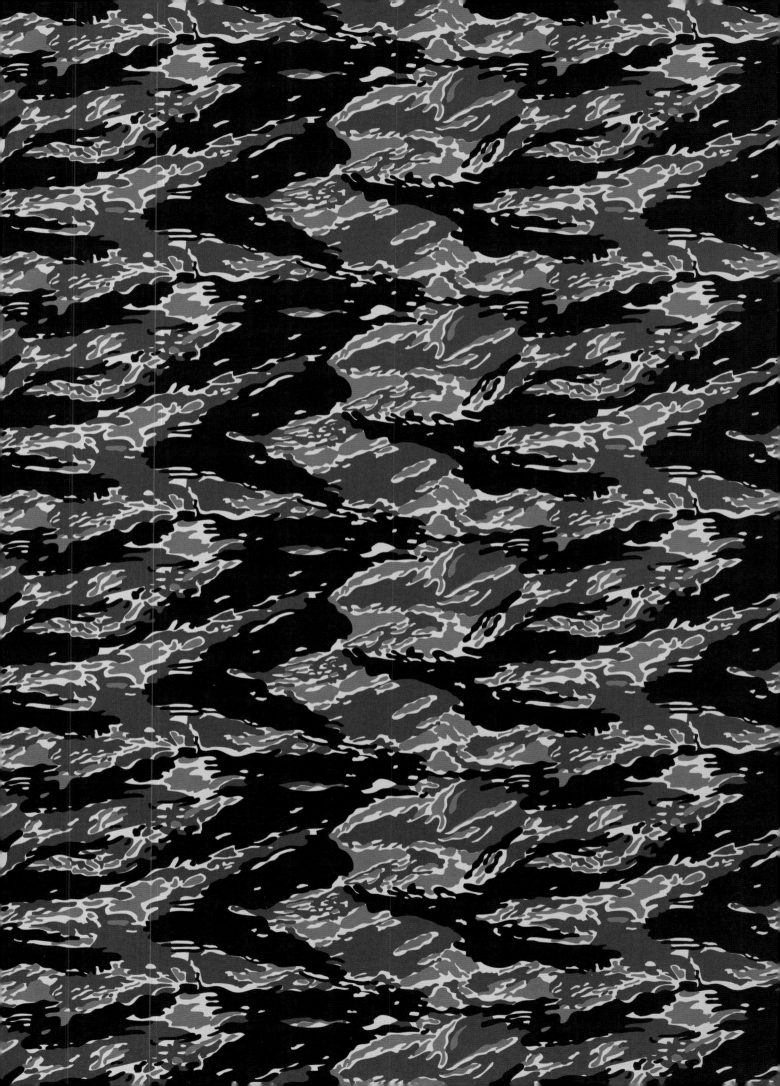

THIS PAGE:
BAPE® X **NUMBER
(N)INE, KANJI**

OPPOSITE PAGE:
CUSTOM ANIMAL
PRINT PATTERN, 2000

FOLLOWING SPREAD:
T-19 X **BAPE**®
SKATEBOARD DECK,
1998

PRECEDING SPREAD:
GENERAL TRIAL CAMO
(R); **NIGO**® (L), 2000

THIS PAGE: **T.I.**, 2006

OPPOSITE PAGE:
BABY MILO® PATTERN,
F/W 2003-2004

133

BELOW:
BAPE® X **U.N.K.L.E.**
VINYL FIGURE, 1999

OPPOSITE PAGE:
JAMES LAVELLE,
1998

THIS PAGE:
OMARION,
2007

OPPOSITE PAGE:
GOOD CHARLOTTE,
2005

THIS PAGE:
DJ SHADOW, 2007

OPPOSITE PAGE;
SHAWN YUE, 2008

FOLLOWING SPREAD,
TERIYAKI BOYZ®,
FROM LEFT TO RIGHT:
ILMARI, **WISE**, **VERBAL**
& **RYO-Z**, 2005

THIS PAGE:
KENJI TAMURA,
2007

OPPOSITE PAGE:
KEN SHIMURA,
2006

BATHING WITH THE APE

Having a hair salon; a café; doing a TV show; the big screen at Harajuku crossing showing content we developed for five minutes every hour, on the hour...doing these different kinds of things is good for our brand.—NIGO®

A BATHING APE® subsists on a diet of raw unpredictability. While retailing clothes and accessories remains the primary commercial engine, the identity of the brand cannot be divorced from the interdependent and often suprising (sub)cultural pursuits NIGO® has engineered around the core business.

The other stuff that fills out this much-expanded universe—both material and immaterial—are not merely add-ons to streetwear. In the past fifteen years, these extracurriculars have variously taken the form of a full-service beauty and hair salon, a café that serves a mix of American and Japanese comfort food, a music label, major media tie-ins, serious architectural sponsorship, a string of wrestling tournaments, the manufacture of collectible vinyl toys, and a curated exhibition program with its own dedicated gallery. Put together, these subassemblies constitute a total BAPE® lifestyle that supplies devotees with both the necessary infrastructure and content.

The range and breadth of these activities naturally grew out of NIGO®'s diverse interests. Often the happy product of circumstance and at times planned to exacting detail, these follow the course of NIGO®'s own youth, education and professional ethic. Already a *fashionista* in junior high school, he prepared for a related career while at college, and managed a fledgling retail business while moonlighting as a stylist and as a DJ. This innate ability to multitask between any number of vocations and hobbies proved crucial, and all that manic energy was redirected once A BATHING APE® became his chief preoccupation.

And being an obsessive-compulsive helps. A notorious collector with a veritable warehouse of toys built around his now-legendary trove of *Planet of the Apes* memorabilia, this propensity to hoard has grown to include everything from records to cars—not to mention an immodest collection of Masamichi Katayama boutiques.

In 2001, A BATHING APE®'s major collaboration with Pepsi Cola marked a turning point for the label. Protective of its underground rep, this tie-in with the soft-drink maker became the company's most visible foray into the mass market. While the move may seem like an abrupt cultural shift given the brand's anti-establishment and anti-populist origins, a decidedly revisionist perspective can argue that it was NIGO® that lent the soda company much-needed streetwise gloss and exposure.

OPPOSITE PAGE:
BAPE GALLERY™, 2002-2005, FEATURING EXHIBIT OF WORKS BY **HAJIME SORAYAMA**, 2002

FOLLOWING SPREAD:
BAPE CUTS™ HARAJUKU, 2002-2007

BAPE CAFE!?

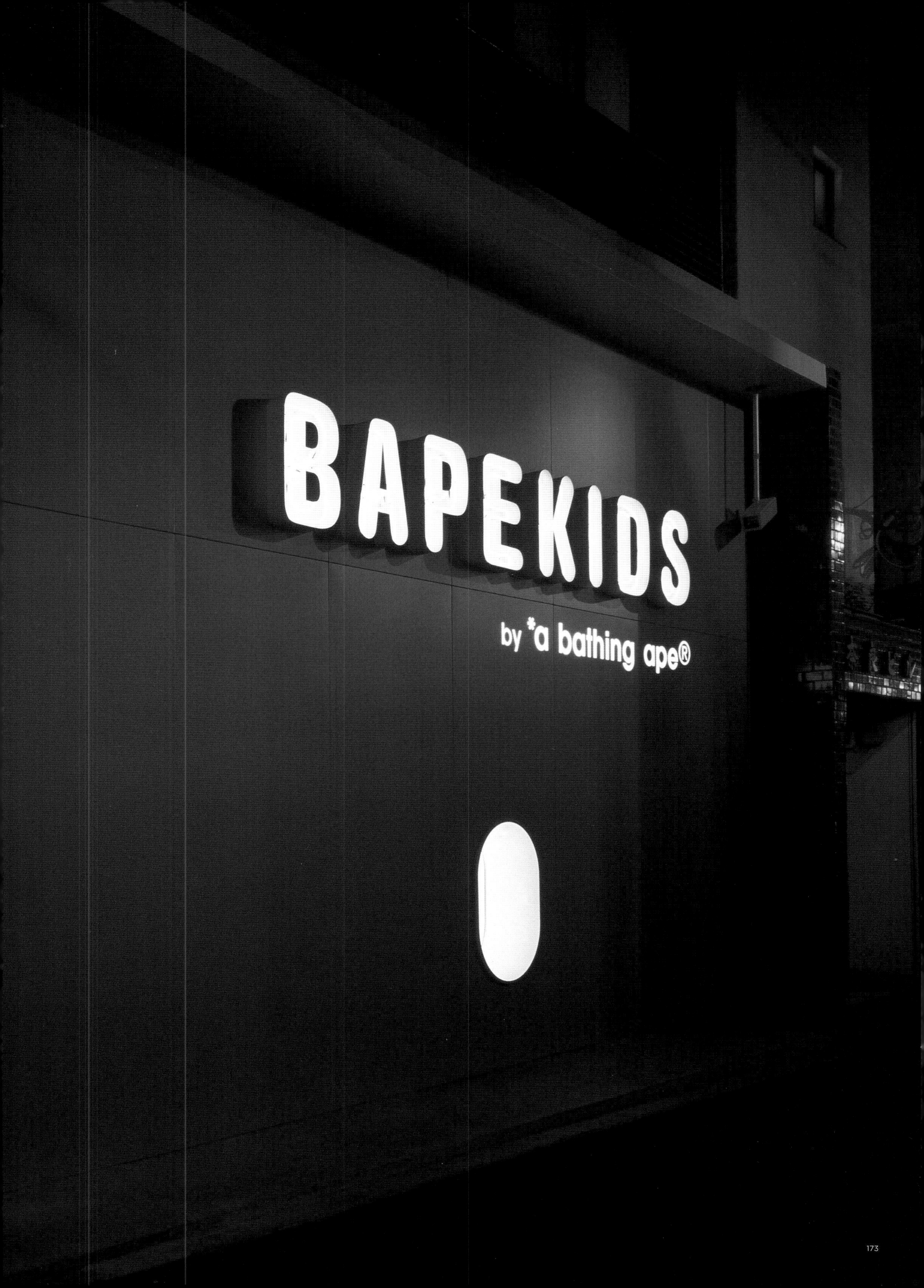
BAPEKIDS
by *a bathing ape®

THIS PAGE:
M.I.A., 2007

PRECEDING SPREAD:
INTERIOR OF **BAPE
KIDS**® HARAJUKU, 2006

THIS PAGE:
BAPE® **TV** LOGO, 2002-
2006

OPPOSITE PAGE:
NIGOLDENEYE
TV PROGRAM FOR
MTV JAPAN, 2006-2008

ONLY

MUSIC TELEVISION

NIGOLDENEYE®

《放送時間》

隔週火曜23:30〜24:00（初回放送）

火曜 26:30〜27:00／水曜 13:30〜14:00／日曜 25:30〜26:00

（リピート放送）

▲
NIGOLDENEYE® グッズはこちら！

http://www.mtvjapan.com/tv/program/rg_nigoldeneye

▲
過去のNIGOLDENEYE®はこちらでチェック！

APESOUNDS®

I was a freshman in high school when I first got into hip-hop. It was all about the American Casual (Amekaji) look at first, but then I got my hands on Adidas' SUPERSTARs and I was hooked. Of course, my love of music was one of the reasons I started a clothing label, but just as Run DMC had me going "laceless Adidas are sick," it's also true that I was hoping younger people would think "APE is sick" while I was producing TERIYAKI BOYZ®—NIGO®

Apesounds® took off as a music label in 1998, and the producers first on board were Kan Takagi and K.U.D.O, two Major Force veterans NIGO® cites as key influences. In a move unprecedented for an apparel brand, a recording studio was built within company quarters—replete with vintage microphones, amps and a drum set. From this, NIGO® paved the way for a professional environment from which his upstart label would later transform the local music industry.

Apesounds® owes much of its worldview to hip-hop. Its clearest representation is the album, *Shadow of the Apesounds*, released at the turn of the millennium. Featuring some of NIGO®'s favorite rappers—Rakim, Biz Markie, Flavor Flav, GZA, and Beatnuts—the album broke new ground in the world of Japanese hip-hop as it succeeded in doing what was heretofore impossible: collaborating with artists from overseas.

NIGO® was as surprised as anyone else of the genuine and effusive welcome that he (and the brand) received in return from the hip-hop community in America—which proved itself to be very open-minded and accepting of new influences. At the time, NIGO® was still very much an outsider, and this recognition was something that he did not anticipate, much less engineer. That A BATHING APE® has gone beyond simply being accepted into the culture to having an influence in its direction in the intervening years was something that was also quite unplanned.

In 2004, *(B)APE SOUNDS* was released, with Pharrell Williams and DJ Shadow as producers, marking NIGO®'s third album. Growing out of a chance encounter with Williams, this creative partnership proved crucial to NIGO® as well, famously leading to the creation of two luxury apparel brands—Billionaire Boys Club and Ice Cream—that have since achieved cult status in the West.

More recently, NIGO®'s attempt to contribute musically to the internationalization of hip-hop has lead to a number of groundbreaking experiments. TERIYAKI BOYZ®—produced by NIGO® and composed of Ilmari and Ryo-Z from Japanese chart-topping rap group Rip Slyme, the rapper Verbal from the hugely popular electronic duo m-flo, and newcomer WISE—is a hip-hop unit unlike any other. With their albums and singles produced by a cross section of global hip-hop royalty, the Boyz have transcended the largely East Asian market that other Japanese pop-groups of the previous two decades were confined to. Performing with Kanye West in 2008, their critical and popular success fulfilled some of the earliest aspirations NIGO® has had for Apesounds®. He didn't want the label to just be a vanity project, and to him, that meant making records that people actually cared about. Now armed with a global reach, and with ever-younger generations convinced of the project, NIGO®—and the beat—goes irrepressibly on.

OPPOSITE PAGE:
A BATHING APE® PRESENTS **BAPE® HEADS TOUR**, 2000, POSTER DESIGNED BY **MANKEY**

FOLLOWING SPREAD: CAMPAIGN BUS FOR **COMMAND Z**, 2000

THIS PAGE:
EXHIBITION OF
FUTURA & **STASH** AT
BAPEXCLUSIVE
AOYAMA,
2000

OPPOSITE PAGE:
BAPE® X **U.N.K.L.E.**
SPRAY CAN CASES
FOR T-SHIRTS

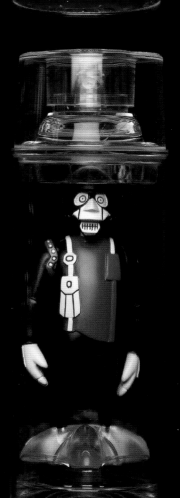

der pressure

wax, moisture and rust

S-025
CMYK

7 24504 01502

APE SHALL NEVER KILL APE APE SHALL NEVER KILL APE APE

BATHING APE
BATHING APE
BAT

BEAST / REIGN SUPREME
BEAST / REIGN SUPREME
BEAS

OFFICIAL
Quality
APEAREL

OFFICIAL
Quality
APEAREL

OFFICIAL
Quality
APEAREL

DANGER: EXTREMELY DOPE, HARMFUL
OR FATAL IF SWALLOWED, BITING HARMFUL
ARTIST PRESSURIZED. PEEP BACK

DANGER: EXTREMELY DOPE, HARMF
OR FATAL IF SWALLOWED, BITING HARMF
ARTIST PRESSURIZED. PEEP BAC

DANGER:
OR FATAL IF
ARTIST PRE

CENTURY 21 ST.
CENTURY 21 ST.

★ 1993 ★
APE SHALL NEVER
KILL APE

BAPE-O-LEUM

BUSY
WORKS

MADE BY GENERAL

DANGER: PRODUCT ENCLOSED EXTREMELY SHRINKABLE
100 PERCENT COTTON . DO NOT IRON IF DECORATED
WASH WHEN NOT SO FRESH.WORD

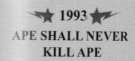

★ 1993 ★
APE SHALL NEVER
KILL APE

BAPE-O-LEUM

BUSY
WORKS

MADE BY GENERAL

DANGER: PRODUCT ENCLOSED EXTREMELY SHRINKABLE
100 PERCENT COTTON . DO NOT IRON IF DECORATED
WASH WHEN NOT SO FRESH.WORD

BAP

DANGER: PRODU
100 PERCENT C
WASH

THIS PAGE:
FLYER FOR WORLDWIDE
BAPE® HEADS SHOW,
1998

OPPOSITE PAGE:
FLYER FOR THE FIRST
WORLDWIDE BAPE®
HEADS SHOW, 1997

FOLLOWING SPREAD:
WORLDWIDE BAPE®
HEADS SHOW, 2000

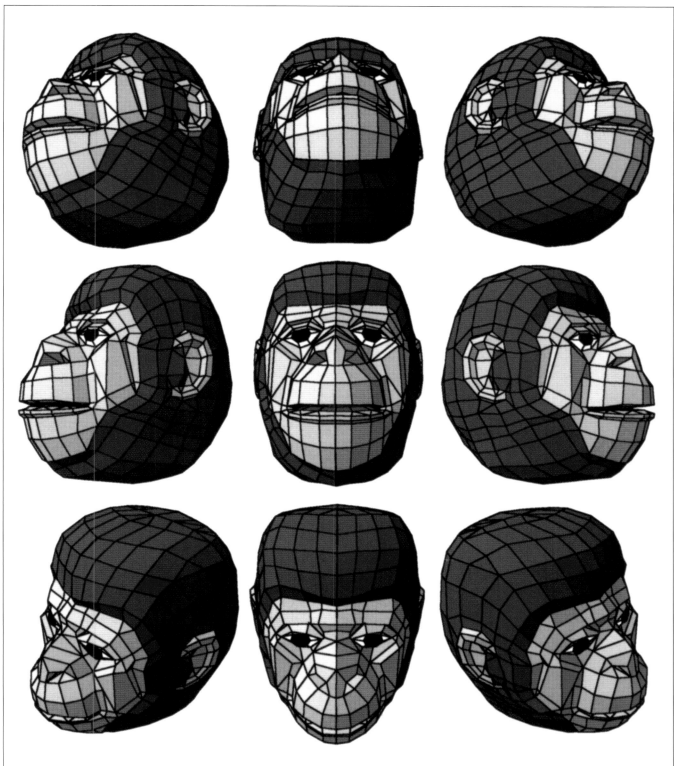

A BATHING APE
presents

WORLDWIDEAPEHEADSSHOW

Starring

.CORNELIUS, SCHA DARA PARR, UA, TOKYO NO.1 SOUL SET, TAKAGI KAN

*A BATHING APE® presents
BAPE® 10th Anniversary Party
2003.11.2(SUN) AT WOMB

EXCLUSIVE LIVE + DJ's

NEPTUNES
CLIPSE
ROSCO P.COLDCHAIN
FAM-LAY
AB LIVA
CIPHA SOUNDS
DJ KAORI

ABOVE:
EVENT FLYER, BAPE®
TENTH ANNIVERSARY
PARTY, 2003

OPPOSITE PAGE:
EVENT FLYER FOR
(B)APE HEADS SHOW
DESIGNED BY MANKEY

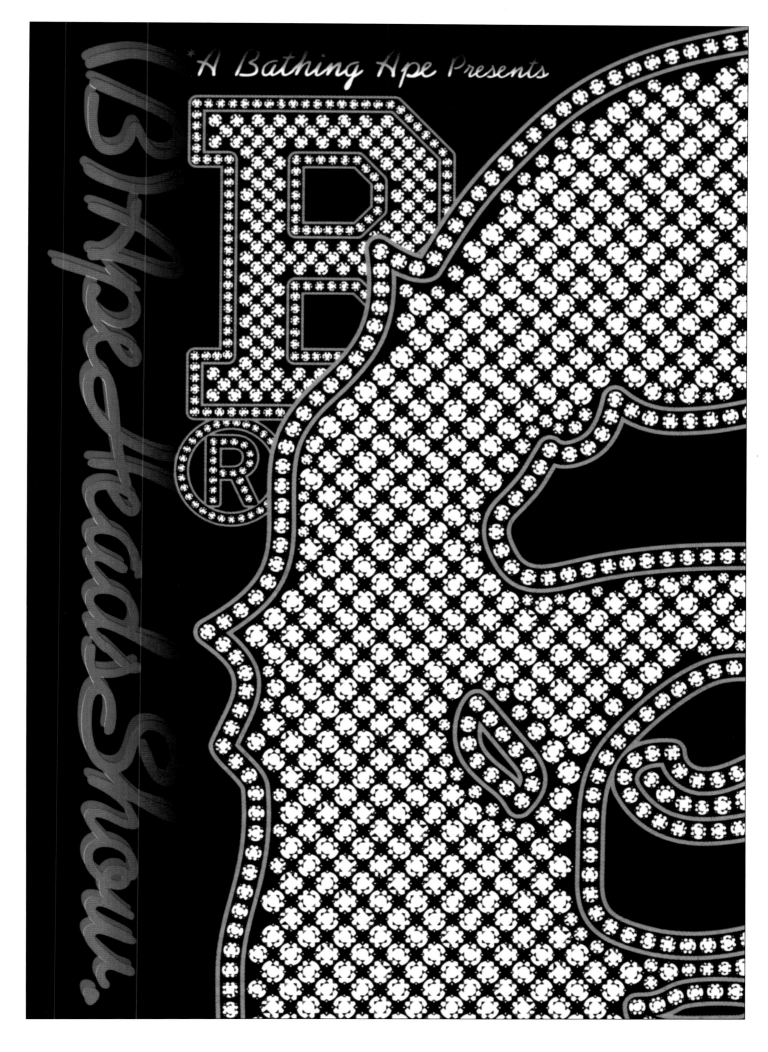

*A Bathing Ape Presents

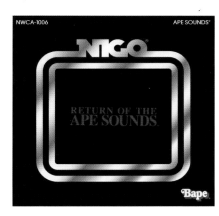

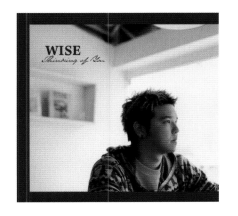

PRECEDING SPREAD:
SELECTION OF CD
COVERS OF **APESOUNDS**®
-PRODUCED SINGLES,
ALBUMS, COMPILATIONS
AND REMIXES

OPPOSITE PAGE:
N.E.R.D. CAMO
PATTERN, 2004

BELOW:
N.E.R.D. PATTERN LOGO
BASEBALL CAP, 2004

ABOVE:
CD COVER FOR
TERIYAKI BOYZ®' *BEEF
OR CHICKEN* ALBUM
(2005), PRODUCED BY
NIGO® WITH THE PAR-
TICIPATION OF **CUT
CHEMIST, CORNELIUS,
DAN THE AUTOMATOR,
ADROCK, DJ SHADOW,
DAFT PUNK, MARK
RONSON, DJ PREMIER,
THE NEPTUNES,
JUST BLAZE,** DESIGNED
BY **SKATETHING**

BELOW:
(B)APESOUNDS®
LOGO DESIGNED BY
ERIC HAZE (2005)

OPPOSITE PAGE:
POSTER FOR THE
TERIYAKI BOYZ®'
*I STILL LOVE H.E.R.
FEAT. KANYE WEST*
CD SINGLE (2008),
PRODUCED AND
FEATURING **KANYE
WEST,** DESIGNED BY
SKATETHING

FOLLOWING SPREAD:
PROMOTIONAL IMAGE
FOR **TERIYAKI BOYZ**®
"BEEF OR CHICKEN
FAIR,"AT **BAPE CAFE!?**®
(2005)

UNIVERSAL MUSIC

I still love H.E.R.

feat. Kanye West

Teriyaki Boyz® New Single

I still love H.E.R. feat. Kanye West

2007.1.24 Out

1.I still love H.E.R. feat. KANYE WEST
2.HeartBreaker (Full Phatt Remix)
3.I still love H.E.R. feat. KANYE WEST (Inst.)

Produced by KANYE WEST

(B)APE SOUNDS® / UNIVERSAL MUSIC

UMCK-5161 ¥1,050 (tax in)

平成14年6月25日発行(毎週火曜日発行) 第48巻・第28号・通算1490号 昭和30年12月16日第三種郵便物認可
週刊プロレス
高山善廣が「PRIDE-21」緊急参戦!?
PRO-WRESTLING 2002
NO.1095
6/25
特別定価490円
ベースボール・マガジン社発行
BASEBALL MAGAZINE SHA
プロレスを
小島プロデューサーの実験、大成功
ALL JAPAN
APEする!

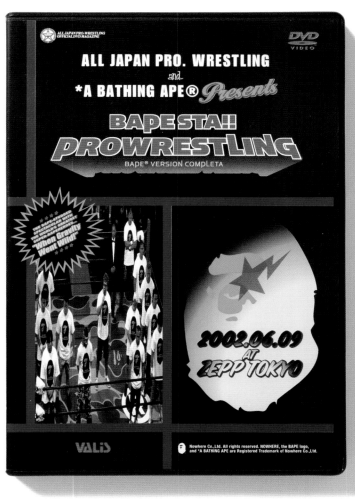

OPPOSITE PAGE:
PROMOTIONAL IMAGE
FOR **BAPE**® X **PEPSI**
COLA, 2001

THIS PAGE:
ILLUSTRATION BY
HAJIME SORAYAMA,
2002

OPPOSITE PAGE:
LOW JACK THREE
WITH **BAPE**® X **PEPSI**
CAMPAIGN NOVELTY,
2001

THIS PAGE:
ILLUSTRATION BY
HAJIME SORAYAMA,
2002

OPPOSITE PAGE:
BAPE® BEER

THIS PAGE:
ILLUSTRATION BY
HAJIME SORAYAMA,
2002

BELOW & OPPOSITE:
LIMITED EDITION T-
SHIRTS & PACKAGING
TO COMMEMORATE
THE FIFTH & SEVENTH
ANNIVERSARIES OF **A
BATHING APE**®, 1998 (L)
& 2000 (R)

OPPOSITE PAGE:
NIGO® IN HONG KONG,
2007

THIS PAGE:
**BAPE STORE® HK
OCTOPUS CARD,** CARD
CASE AND LANYARD,
2007

BELOW:
LEATHER JACKET,
S/S 2001

OPPOSITE PAGE:
PROMOTIONAL MATCH-
BOOK FOR **BAPE
STORE**® HARAJUKU,
ADJACENT TO OMOTE-
SANDO HILLS, WHICH
OPENED IN JANUARY
2008

BELOW: LEATHER
DOWN JACKET,
F/W 2000-2001

OPPOSITE PAGE:
BABY MILO®, DESIGNED
BY **MANKEY**, 2008

OPPOSITE PAGE:
MAYUKO IWASA, 2004

THIS PAGE:
LIMITED EDITION T-
SHIRT FOR *WEEKLY
PLAYBOY*, DESIGNED
BY **MANKEY**, 2004

BELOW:
BABY MILO® X **KAWS**,
2005

OPPOSITE PAGE:
TOP TO BOTTOM,
BAPE® X **KAWS**, F/W
2005-2006; S/S 2005;
S/S 2005

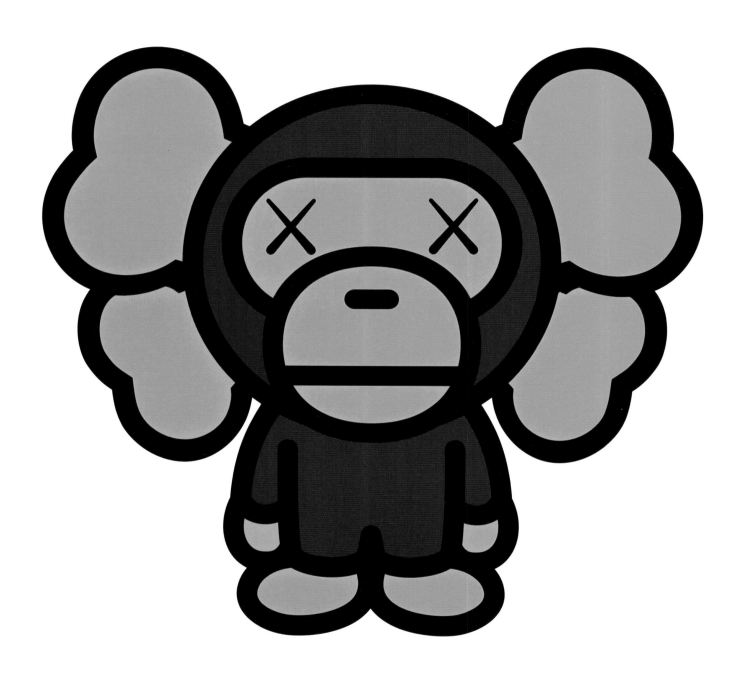

   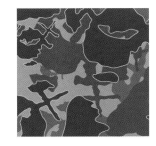

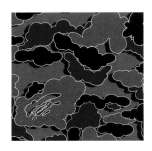 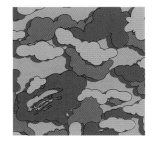 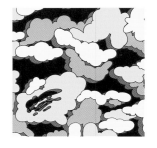 

  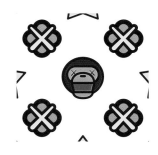 

THIS PAGE:
BAPE® X **KAWS** PAT-
TERNS, S/S 2005-S/S
2006

OPPOSITE PAGE:
JAY-Z, 2005

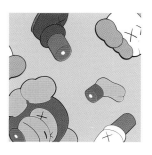 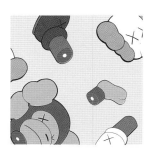 

THIS PAGE:
INTERIOR OF **NIGO**®'s
ATELIER IN TOKYO

OPPOSITE PAGE:
BAPE® X **KAWS**
PATTERNS, 2005

キープ・ヤ

ヘッド・アップ

さんた

人生、
上り坂もあれば、
下り坂もあるさ
だから

FAKE FUR AND VINYL UPHOLSTERED CHAIR WITH ARMS -GARY PANTER

BELOW:
BAPE® X **GARY PANTER**
NYLON JACKET, F/W
2004-2005

OPPOSITE PAGE:
PATTERN DESIGNED
FOR **BAPE**® BY **GARY**
PANTER

THIS PAGE:
BAPE® X **GARY PANTER**
PYJAMA TOP AND
BOTTOM, F/W 2004-
2005

OPPOSITE PAGE:
PATTERN DESIGNED
FOR **BAPE®** BY **GARY
PANTER**

OPPOSITE PAGE:
MEMBERS' EDITION OF
SHARK PARKA, WORN
BY **NIGO**® AT HIS
TOKYO ATELIER, 2006

THIS PAGE:
SHARK PARKAS, F/W
2005-2006 TO S/S
2007

OPPOSITE PAGE:
TIGER PARKA, WORN
BY KANYE WEST, 2006

THIS PAGE:
TIGER PARKAS, F/W
2006-2007 TO F/W
2007-2008

OPPOSITE PAGE:
THE INAUGURAL
ISSUE OF *BAPE PAPER*,
FEATURING **EMIRI
HENMI,** JUNE 1999

THIS PAGE:
ISSUES 1 THROUGH 8
OF THE RELAUNCHED
BAPE PAPER, FROM
FEBRUARY 2006
THROUGH MARCH
2008, FEATURING
MAYUKO IWASA(1),
YU ABIRU (2),
MISAKO YASUDA (3),
AKI HOSHINO (4),
YUKO OGURA (5),
JUN NATSUKAWA (6),
ERIKA TODA (7), &
SHOKO HAMADA (8)

KICKS

In a way, BAPE STA™ sneakers happened by accident, so I did not expect them to have such a strong following in and outside Japan. Let's just say the line was a product of last resort that made a good turn for the better. We are not a proper sportswear manufacturer but a fashion brand, so the sneakers are merely a component of the seasonal collections, but they definitely set the trend for colorful sneakers.—NIGO®

The decision to remake a familiar athletic shoe from the 1980s in impossibly bright, glossy colors resulted in one of the most recognizable product lines that A BATHING APE® has ever created. Launched just at the moment Japan's sneaker boom went into overdrive, the old-school appeal of BAPE STA™ distinguished themselves from the techy, streamlined look that characterized athletic footwear of the mid- to late-1990s. Introduced in the midst of a retro counterrevolution in sneaker design, and with each new colorway issued in such limited quantities, the STAs™ became a domestic hit.

Despite their no-frills design, the popularity of the shoes in Japan were further bolstered by a little retailing gadgetry, courtesy of NIGO®'s long-time architectural collaborator Masamichi Katayama. Foot Soldier, the original concept store for Ape footwear opened in the chic shopping enclave of Daikanyama in 2001. Life-size cutouts of armed primates are repeated across the black interior walls of the ground-floor shop, their anthrophomorphic silhouettes marching on the checkerboard of a multihued carpet. But the consistent draw—and the defining characteristic of many BAPE® stores hence—is a large automated display, encased in glass and visible from within and without. Built to the industrial standards of airport conveyor belts by D. Brain Co., Ltd., the interlocking steel track featured a perpetual parade of sneakers.

For BAPE® addicts outside Japan, the existence of STAs™ soon passed from rumor to legend. The Beastie Boys, N.E.R.D., Snoop Dogg, Jay-Z, Usher, Kanye West, and a host of other hip-hop V.I.P.'s began rocking them not only in private, but on stage, on MTV, and even in the lyrics of their songs. All this high-powered advocacy surged the shoe's growing reputation as a status symbol. The 2005 arrival of BAPE® in New York was hastened in no small part by an appetite for STAs™, and kids regularly form long lines around the SoHo store once word of shipment drop-dates from Japan are leaked by sneaker blogs.

One unintended irony was that the formula for STA™ success migrated back to the major athletic shoe companies. The once subversive application of enameled fabric and patent leather in high-contrast colors has become a feature of sneaker lines both large and small. Never one to skulk away from a challenge, NIGO® reacted with characteristic good humor and ingenuity, and the subsequent release of limited editions done in collaboration with Brooklyn-based KAWS, and later partnerships with DC and Marvel comics have assured the preeminence of the STA™ and its value to consumers as well as collectors.

Clearly the most visible, BAPE STAs™ are not the only examples of Ape footwear. A BATHING APE® continues to launch new styles and experiments with other brands, the most notable of which include the all-leather Manhunt in 1999, and subsequent tie-ups with Adidas.

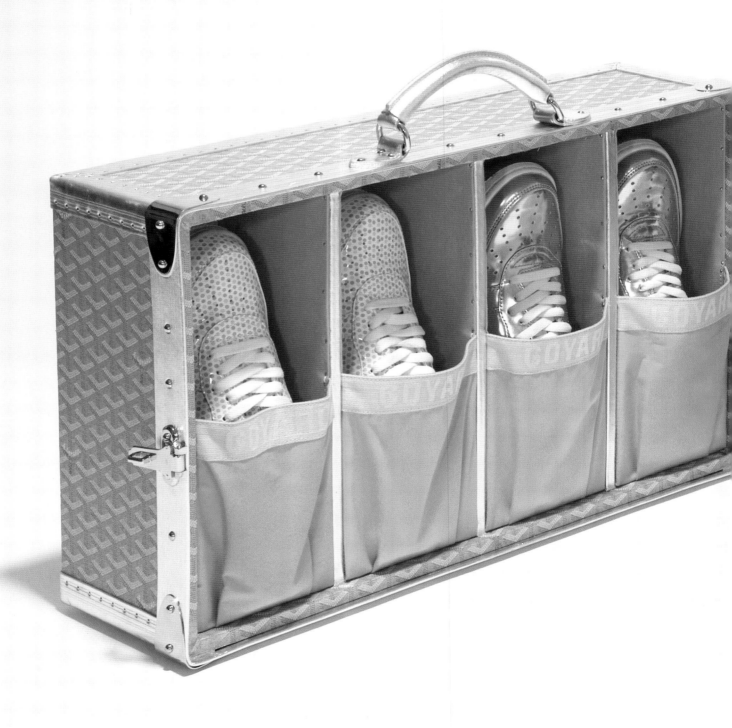

THIS PAGE:
**FOOT SOLDIER
DAIKANYAMA** (2001-
2005), DESIGNED WITH
**MASAMICHI KATAYA-
MA/ WONDERWALL**

267

OPPOSITE PAGE:
KANYE WEST LIMITED-
EDITION **BAPE STA**™,
F/W 2006-2007

THIS PAGE:
KANYE WEST, 2006

FOLLOWING SPREAD:
LEFT PAGE, INTERIOR
VIEW OF **BAPE STORE**®
HONG KONG (2006),
DESIGNED WITH
MASAMICHI KATAYAMA/
WONDERWALL

269

THIS PAGE:
BAPE STA™ CUSTOM
DESIGNED BY **VERBAL**
OF **M-FLO**, WITH
SWAROVSKI
CRYSTALS, 2004

OPPOSITE PAGE:
POLKA DOTS **BAPE
STA**™, 2006

LINES OF DESCENT

When I see the world's fashion mega-brands, their product lines are often limited to men's and women's collections. I thought my label had grown into a status worthy of a similar, binary equation, so I simplified and integrated A BATHING APE® to just the men's and women's lines. What the customer ultimately looks for is A BATHING APE®, and this often boils down to "a brown and flesh-colored monkey."—NIGO®

In the past, A BATHING APE® was subdivided into a number of secondary lines with specific thematic labels, such as the women's BAPY® and APEE® brands, or the more character-driven BABY MILO®. These collections sometimes existed as discreet realms within the larger BAPE® universe, often with their own freestanding stores, and with unabashedly loyal fan bases.

The strategic plan to reorganize the disparate parts of A BATHING APE® began in 2007 when the label switched gears and transitioned to a simpler brand concept. By formally maintaining only the men's and women's collections under A BATHING APE®, NIGO® firmly believes that after fifteen years, the label has grown into a brand that fits neatly into the tried-and-true business model of most international fashion and luxury makes.

This decision to consolidate the major adult apparel lines does not however mean that the choice and diversity that NIGO® intended for the BAPE® consumer is diminished. Well into its second decade, the conception of A BATHING APE® as a bearer of surprise and delight is even more evident now, as the range of apparel, from basic items to outfits for special occasions (such as traditional Japanese attire), is much expanded to accommodate a catalogue of geographic, generational and lifestyle preferences that were not necessarily anticipated at the brand's inception. At the heart of the BAPE® cannon, fashion had always been intended as a modality tightly interlocked with a myriad of other subcultures —including music, hobbies, art, architecture and design—and the flexibility to adapt to changing consumer preferences remains a keystone of the brand's worldview.

OPPOSITE PAGE:
EXTERIOR VIEW OF
BAPY® AOYAMA
(2002-2007),
DESIGNED WITH
**MASAMICHI KATAYA-
MA/ WONDERWALL**

FOLLOWING SPREAD:
BAPY®, 2001

THIS SPREAD:
AKIKO KIKUCHI (L),
NANA UCHIDA (R) FOR
BAPY®, 2001

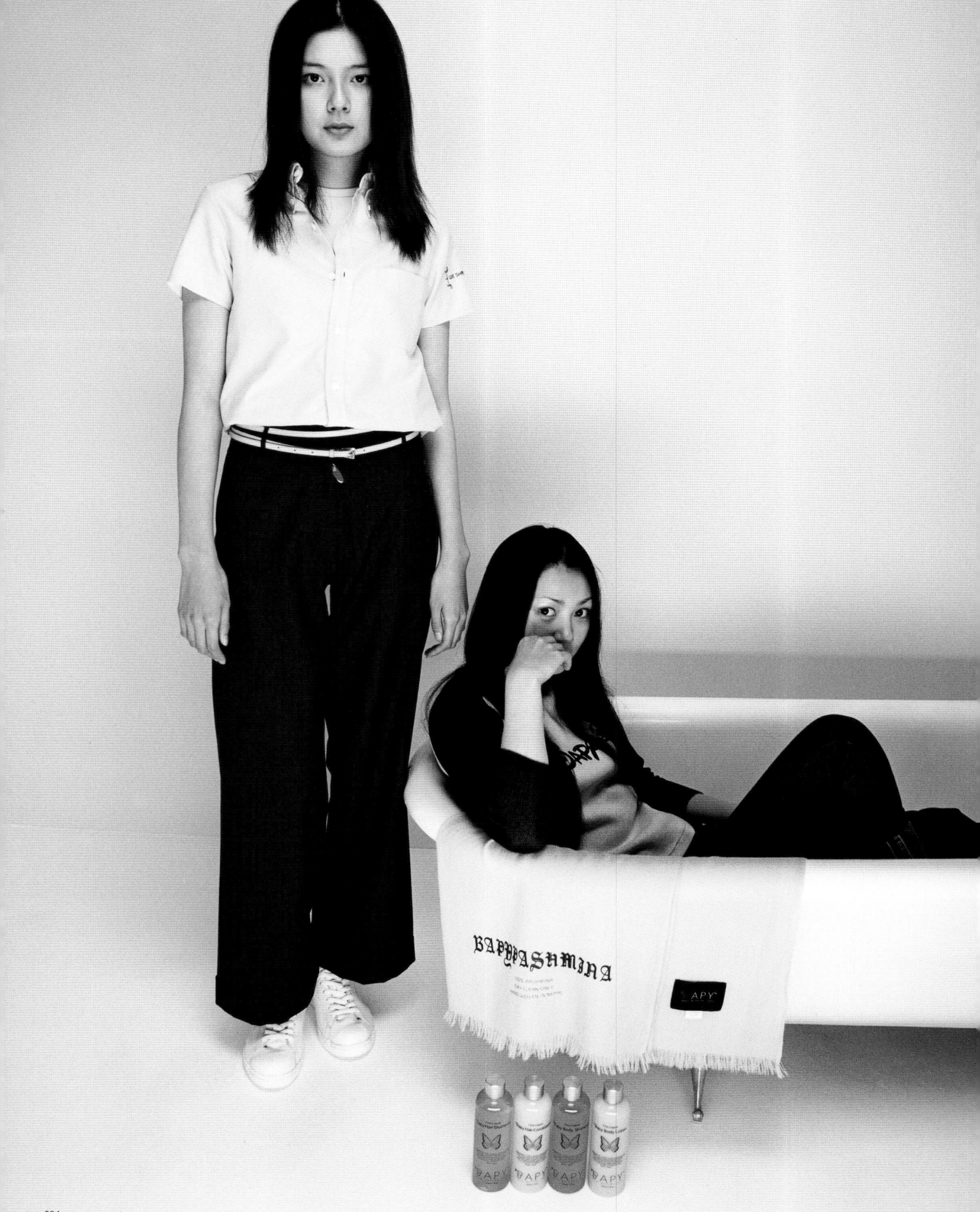

THIS PAGE:
BAPY® 2002.

OPPOSITE PAGE:*
BAPY® 2002

FOLLOWING SPREAD:
ENTRANCE & INTERIOR
VIEWS OF **BABY MILO®**
STORE, (2002-2006),
DESIGNED WITH
**MASAMICHI KATAYA-
MA/ WONDERWALL**

bapy

appeal

*BAPYTIME

BUSY WORKING LADY

TOKYO EDITION

UPDATE YOUR LOOK

Sofia Jeffner

FASHION
BEAUTY&HEALTH
MUSIC&BOOKS
ARTS&MOVIES
DINING
WHAT'S HOT?

WE SHALL ...BAPY T

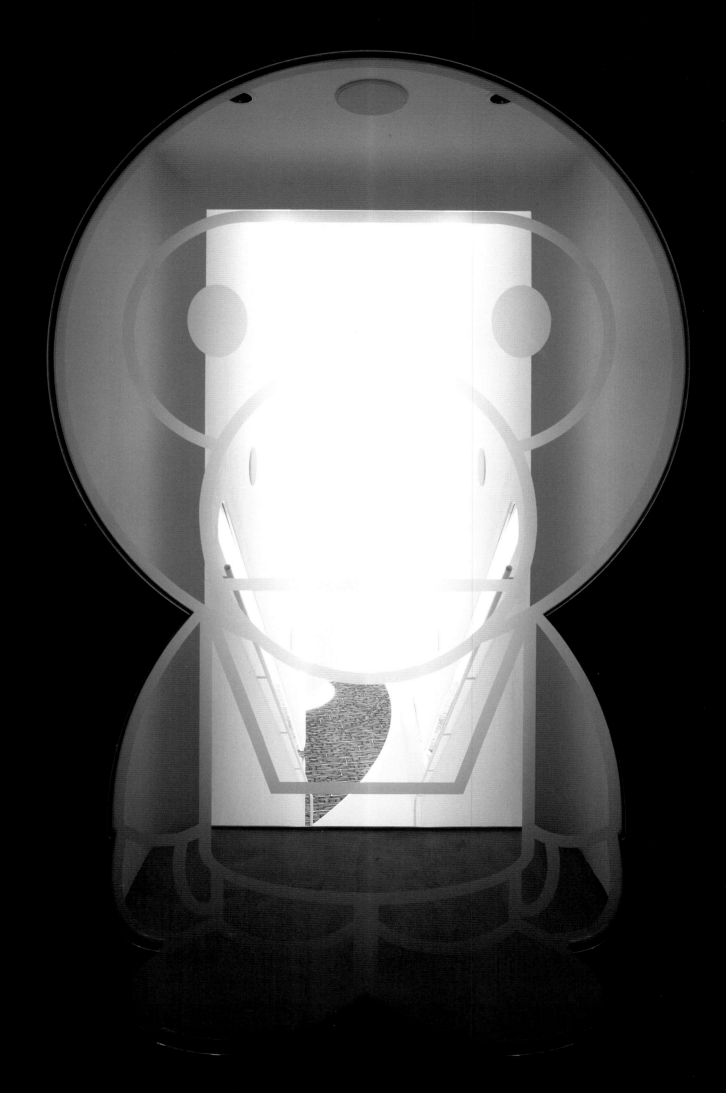

THIS PAGE:
JUN NATSUKAWA,
2005

OPPOSITE PAGE:
BABY MILO® ALPHABET
CHARACTERS,
DESIGNED BY MANKEY

MILO
マイロ
まいろ

LISA
リサ
りさ

BEAR
ベアー
くま

CAT
キャット
ねこ

DOG
ドッグ
いぬ

ELEPHANT
エレファント
ぞう

FOX
フォックス
きつね

GIRAFFE
ジラフ
きりん

HIPPO
ヒッポ
かば

IBEX
アイベックス
やぎ

JACKAL
ジャッカル
じゃっかる

KOALA
コアラ
こあら

LION
ライオン
らいおん

MOUSE
マウス
ねずみ

NEWT
ニュート
いもり

OCTOPUS
オクトパス
たこ

PANTHER
パンサー
ひょう

QUAIL
クエール
うずら

RABBIT
ラビット
うさぎ

SQUIRREL
スクィレル
りす

TURTLE
タートル
かめ

UNICORN
ユニコーン
ゆにこーん

VULTURE
ヴァルチャー
はげわし

WALRUS
ウールルス
せいうち

X
エックス
えっくす

YAK
ヤック
やく

ZEBRA
ゼブラ
しまうま

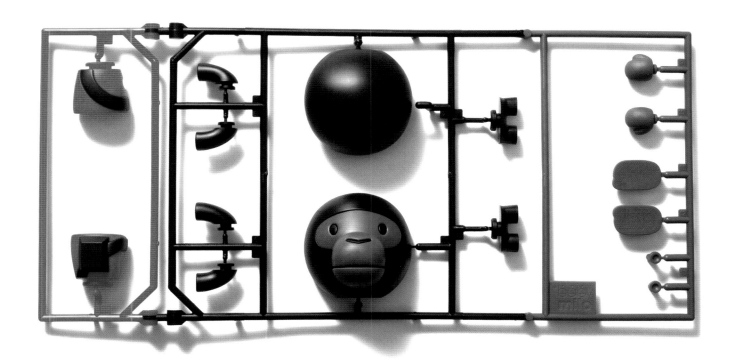

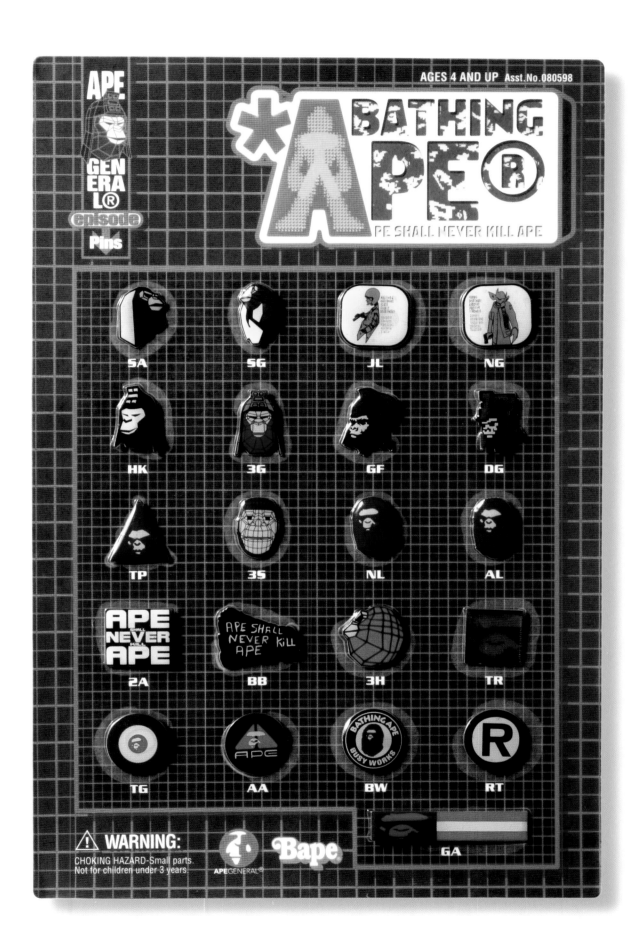

PREVIOUS SPREAD:
ART DIRECTION BY
ATSUSHI OKUBO, 2002

THIS SPREAD:
PACKAGING FOR **MAGIC
PLATES** (1998-2005).
EACH BOX CONTAINS 5
PLASTIC "MAGIC
PLATES" WHICH
REQUIRE BAKING IN AN
OVEN TO SHRINK TO
THE SIZE OF KEYRING
HOLDERS

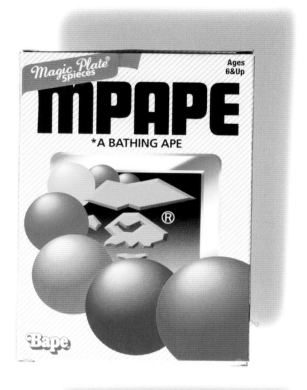
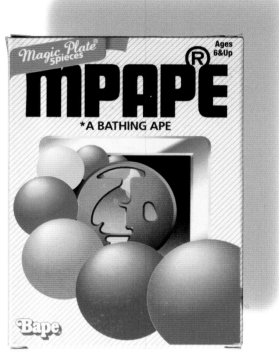

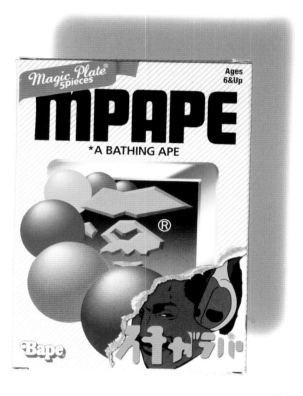

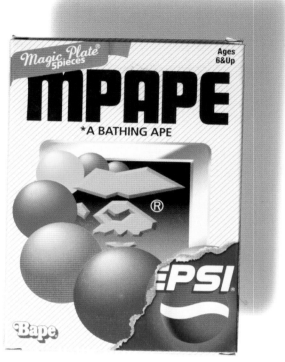

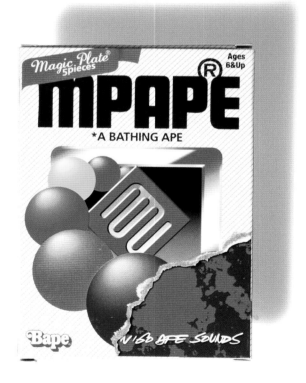

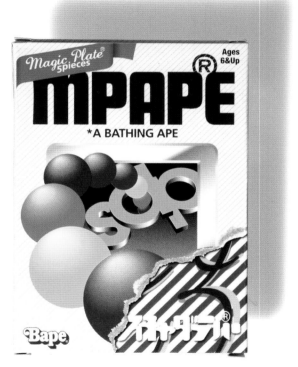

BELOW:
BAPE® LUNCH BOX,
2007

OPPOSITE PAGE:
BAPE® *KINTARO AME*, A
CYLINDRICAL HARD
CANDY THAT REVEALS
BAPE® ICONS WHEN IT
IS SNAPPED IN PIECES,
2000

OPPOSITE PAGE:
NIGO® IN THE ATELIER
OF CHISO YUZEN IN
KYOTO, 2001

THIS PAGE:
YURI MORISHITA, 2008

THIS PAGE:
SPECIAL ITEMS FROM
A COLLECTOR'S BOX
ISSUED ON THE 11TH
ANNIVERSARY OF
A BATHING APE®

OPPOSITE PAGE:
BAPE STA™ ISSUED ON
THE 11TH ANNIVERSARY
OF **A BATHING APE**®

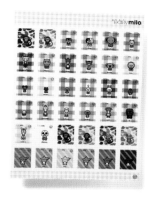

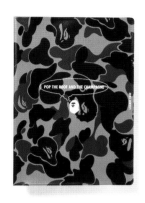

THE EARLY DAYS

When I first opened the store, it was a total blast. All my friends were there and something cool was happening every single day. Back then, we were just slackers to a lot of people. But each of us owned a store, and we were all turning a profit. This seems improbable now, but it happened right there in Harajuku.—NIGO®

Rewind to the Tokyo of the early 1990s. The asset price bubble that fueled the excesses of the previous decade had just collapsed, and the recession that followed in its wake had an instantaneous and crippling effect on cultural production. In fashion and its allied trades, the contraction in the economy forced an untimely end to the "Designer Boom" that defined the Tokyo high street for much of the 1980s. The pervasive feeling of unease and uncertainty afflicted even the most unflappable, and flash-frozen in amber, the fashion industry seemed in the doldrums. The salvation promised by the internet—and the reversal of fortune tied with the rise of the "New Economy" a decade later—was still very much a rumor.

But in Harajuku, a precinct in Shibuya Ward defined by the intersection of Omotesando and Meiji-Dori, a tentative sense of revival was afoot. In its warren of side-streets, ancient storefronts and crumbling housing complexes, a scrappy group of designer/proprietors, many of them looking fresh out of high school, began to open apparel stores—one by one by one.

One could not properly call them boutiques, but even before opening hours, shoppers would form long lines at the steps of these shoebox-size stores. Enterprising magazine editors took to calling this retailing boom-let the "Ura-Harajuku Movement," and the semantic hype was soon matched by its transformative effect on fashion and youth culture. With "identity" as their organizing principle, and the "limited-edition" as its vehicle, the constituent parts of this movement introduced design and retailing concepts not yet seen in Japan—or anywhere else.

At the heart of all this was the team of NIGO® and UNDERCOVER's Jun Takahashi. Flanked by like-minded friends, they formed a self-sustaining and interdependent community. Functioning like a small village with shared interests and approximate values, personalities who in other contexts would ordinarily be rivals convened—and often collaborated. They magnified their influence beyond the confines of fashion by engaging music, media and other design disciplines with unprecedented pluralism. In the hypercompetitive condition of global fashion, the Harajuku group favored cross-pollination as an alternative to fierce competition. The collaborative products of this guild—christened "Double-Name" goods—migrated to the high street, and in time, even transformed the relationships between established mega-brands and fashion combines.

It was this particular environment from which A BATHING APE® emerged. Designers like NIGO® eschewed the anti-populist orientation of high fashion, but valued the premium it placed on innovation and rationing supply. With streetwear as their medium of choice, the denizens of Harajuku village worked hard at creating a haven for self-expression within what was then a homogenous marketplace.

Looking back, some of the earliest artifacts of A BATHING APE® provide some of the best examples of this new conception of streetwear. Basic items distinguished by their mass-produced antecedents by superior manufacture, they give evidence of an unhindered, creative energy. Initially conceived without a deep, specialized knowledge of fashion and industrial processes, the ingenuity of these designs lie in a subversion of apparel conventions and haberdashery details. With not a little deconstruction, the Apehead tags so associated with the brand were first affixed to the leading edges of t-shirt sleeves during this period, and tinkering with zippers, rivets, buttons, pockets and other elements were not far behind. This intimate, attentive approach to craft has survived to this day, and they play no small part in bringing NIGO® and his peers to industry acclaim. This spirit is crucial to the BAPE® formula, and its founding principles have survived the subsequent decline of Harajuku for the brand to take on the world.

OPPOSITE PAGE:
BAPE® CAMOUFLAGE SHIRT, F/W 1996-1997

OPPOSITE PAGE:
ORIGINAL DENIM, S/S
1995

THIS PAGE:
SWEATSHIRT, S/S 1995

FOLLOWING SPREAD:
SWEATER, 1995

ngland

RY APE

"m very ape
nd very nice"

ONE
SIZE

OPPOSITE PAGE:
INVITATION FOR
A BATHING APE®
EXHIBITION, F/W
1997-1998

BELOW:
CATALOGUE WITH
TOTE BAG, S/S 1999

No. 000025

THIS SPREAD:
CLOCKWISE FROM
LEFT, BOY SCOUT
SHIRT, F/W 1998-1999 ;
STADIUM JACKET. F/W
1995-1996; "DISCO"
SHIRT, F/W 1995-1996

OPPOSITE PAGE:
CAMOUFLAGE JACKET
WITH DETACHABLE
HOOD AND MASK, F/W
1998-1999

THIS PAGE:
BAPE® RECORD
PLAYER, 1998

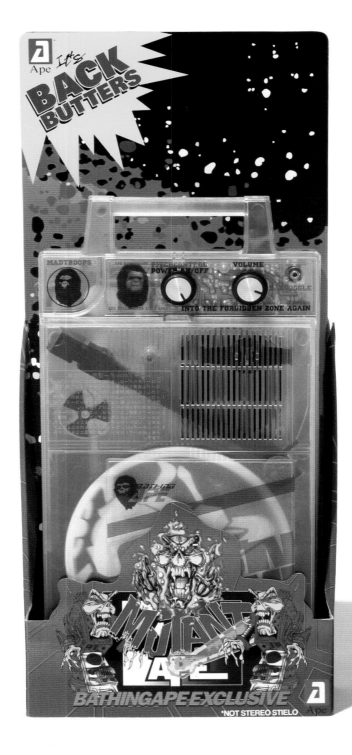

OPPOSITE PAGE:
SHOPPING BAG FOR
TECHNIQUE SHOP
DESIGNED BY **STASH**,
1997-1998

BELOW:
SHOP CARD FOR
CONCEPT SHOP,
DESIGNED BY **STASH**,
1996-1998

CONCEPT SHOP
PRODUCTS FROM BEYOND

that which exists in the mind as the product of careful mental activity:
IDEA THOUGHT IMAGE CONCEPTION PERCEPTION

3-28-11 NARA BLDG. 4F JINGUMAE SHIBUYA-KU TOKYO 150 JAPAN
03/3478/9995

FOLLOWING SPREAD:
BAPE® X **STEPHEN
EINHORN** FIRE GARDEN,
1999 (L); **BAPE®** X
CANADIAN SWEATER
"COWICHAN"
SWEATER, F/W 1996-
1997

337

BATTLESPACE

Katayama is one of a few remarkable designers capable of realizing my ideas no matter how ambiguous my instructions might be. He is very much in demand right now, with many other clients, but I'm proud to say that we began collaborating very early in his career.—NIGO®

By the late 1990s, the domestic distribution of A BATHING APE® products were done largely through a network of "select" shops—independent fashion boutiques that sold hard-to-find labels. Faced with respectable but less-than-stellar receipts, NIGO® made a command decision that all BAPE® goods would henceforth be sold exclusively in his own shops.

So it was In 1998—the thirtieth anniversary of the original *Planet of the Apes*—that NIGO® added architectural patron to his growing list of titles, finding a kindred spirit in Masamichi Katayama, a young interior designer from Okayama prefecture also motivated by an unfettered sense of play. Now at the helm of Wonderwall, Katayama had at the time been a principal at another firm when he was first tapped to renovate the original shop that A BATHING APE® shared with UNDERCOVER. Katayama remembers that he'd first met NIGO® through a mutual acquaintance, and was surprised that they'd hit it off so quickly.

Carved out of a basement in one of the narrow alleys of Harajuku, A Bathing Ape Busy Work Shop® was the label's prototype boutique. NIGO® and Katayama would revise the entry sequence and tweak the interior three years later, but the original concept was essentially unchanged. Shoppers descended from the street through a stair parallel with the curb, traversed a narrow forecourt, and entered the Work Shop® through a concrete doorway.

Katayama's adaptable brand of modernism resonated with the best qualities of Japanese practice: precise, fastidious, and well proportioned, and the store interior showcases a mania for reflective surfaces and misdirection.

Avoiding the conventional approach of maximizing all available space for retail, the collection itself is seemingly relegated to the margins of the program. Hung along a wall-length chrome dowel, atop a series of shiny stainless-steel tables, or else inside glazed hermetic cases, these displays form the perimeter of an open, rectangular space. At one of their first meetings, Katayama recalls that NIGO® wanted to only "have about twenty garments in the store, which really shocked me. At the time I thought it was such an anti-commercial statement, but at the same time, I was certain that we would create something very special. It was very unusual to give up some of the selling space for what was essentially a wide corridor, but it was necessary to accommodate a large number of customers." He effectively created something that was at once a jeweled box for merchandise and a gathering place for youth. Katayama remarked that the Busy Work Shop® was so popular that on some nights it remained a destination long after the daily supply of limited-edition goods was exhausted.

1999 saw NIGO® and Katayama on their second collaboration in Tokyo, inserting the first Bapexclusive store into the ground floor of an existing two-story building in nearby Aoyama. At the time, NIGO®'s decision to break out of the old 'hood and migrate to what were then more "upscale" digs was interpreted by some in Harajuku as a controversial move. But it was to be a necessary one if NIGO®'s expansive ambitions for the brand were to be realized.

Stores all over Japan followed in quick succession, and in the last decade, Katayama has designed or renovated over fifty locations for A BATHING APE®, fanning out of Japan with outposts in Hong Kong, London, New York, and Los Angeles. Ideas that first found expression at the inaugural Harajuku shop are now found in BAPE® stores the world over, the distinctive, shimmering iconography of an architectural program that neither collaborator professes to be terribly conscious about.

OPPOSITE PAGE:
**BUSY WORK SHOP®
NAGOYA** (1998),
DESIGNED WITH
**MASAMICHI KATAYA-
MA/ WONDERWALL**

FOLLOWING SPREAD:
INTERIOR VIEW OF
NOWHERE HARAJUKU
(1998), DESIGNED WITH
**MASAMICHI KATAYA-
MA/ WONDERWALL**

NOWHERE

THIS SPREAD:
VIEW OF **BUSY WORK SHOP®** **OSAKA** (1998), DESIGNED WITH **MASAMICHI KATAYA-MA/ WONDERWALL**

FOLLOWING SPREAD:
EXTERIOR VIEW OF **BUSY WORK SHOP® FUKUOKA** (1999), DESIGNED WITH **MASAMICHI KATAYA-MA/ WONDERWALL**

SENDAI (1998),
DESIGNED WITH
**MASAMICHI KATAYA-
MA/ WONDERWALL**

KYOTO (1999),
DESIGNED WITH
**MASAMICHI KATAYA-
MA/ WONDERWALL**

*A BATHING APE
"BUSY WORK SHOP"

THIS SPREAD:
VIEW OF **BUSY WORK
SHOP**® **MAEBASHI**
(1999)

DESIGNED WITH
**MASAMICHI KATAYA-
MA/ WONDERWALL**

THIS PAGE:
INTERIOR VIEW OF
BUSY WORK SHOP®
HONG KONG (1999-2005),
DESIGNED WITH
MASAMICHI KATAYA-
MA/ WONDERWALL

OPPOSITE PAGE:
INTERIOR VIEW OF
BUSY WORK SHOP®
HARAJUKU (2001),
DESIGNED WITH
MASAMICHI KATAYA-
MA/ WONDERWALL

*A BATHING APE "

THIS SPREAD:
INTERIOR VIEWS OF
**BUSY WORK SHOP®
NEW YORK** (2004),
DESIGNED WITH
**MASAMICHI KATAYA-
MA/ WONDERWALL**

FOLLOWING SPREAD:
BAPE STORE® SHIBUYA
(2007), DESIGNED WITH
**MASAMICHI KATAYA-
MA/ WONDERWALL**

SPECIAL!
JAPAN'S
HOTTEST
ICONS

June 2005

Interview

GOES TO **TOKYO**
WITH KARL LAGERFELD

DIAMOND
CRAZY
SUPER
STAR

NIGO

BY PHARRELL
WILLIAMS

UTADA BY
NICK RHODES

PUFFY AMIYUMI
BY SELMA BLAIR

CHIAKI KURIYAMA
BY DARYL HANNAH

TOM FORD
ON TADAO
ANDO

TAKESHI
KANESHIRO
BY INGRID
SISCHY

YOKO ONO
& TAKASHI
MURAKAMI

ABOVE:
THE COVER OF THE
JUNE 2005 ISSUE OF
INTERVIEW MAGAZINE,
EDITED BY KARL
LAGERFELD

MADE BY HUMANS

To everybody who appears in or contributed to this book, or gave us permission to use their material. To all of the people who have worked with me, supported me, or helped me over the last 15 years. To all the fans of A BATHING APE®

Thank you!—NIGO®, A.K.A. BAPE® General

INDEX

PHOTO CREDITS

© Jimmy Cohrssen: 2, 7; © P. M. Ken: 8; © Mari Amita: 18; © P. M. Ken: 28; © Shawn Mortensen: 34; © Ichiro Shiomi: 37; © Kozo Takayama: 39, 42-43; © Keisuke Nagase, A Bathing Ape® 2005 A/W Collection/ Takarajimasha, Inc.: 45; Naoaki Matsumoto, Courtesy of *Free & Easy* Magazine/ East Rights, December 2003: 50; P.M. Ken Courtesy of *Relax* Magazine House, October 2001 Oct: 51; © Makoto Nakagawa: 59; P. M. Ken for *Relax* Magazine/Magazine House, January 2004: 60; Marvin Scott Jarrett, Courtesy of *NYLON Guys* Magazine: 66© P.M.Ken: 67; © Keisuke Naito, Bape Kids® by A Bathing Ape® 2007 A/W Collection/Takarajimasha, Inc.: 74, 77; P.M. Ken: 78; © Hiroshi Nomura, Smart Max/ Takarajimasha, Inc., August 2004: 87; P.M. Ken, Courtesy of *Vogue Nippon*/Conde Nast Japan, October 2004: 90; Osamu Matsuo, Courtesy of *Shoesmaster*, Vol. 7: 91; © Hidetomo Abe, Smart/ Takarajimasha,Inc., May 2000: 112; Hiromix, Courtesy of *Thrill* Magazine, February 2000: 117; Wataru Nishida, Courtesy of *Ollie* Magazine, September 2006: 118; © Keisuke Naito: 120-121; P.M. Ken, A Bathing Ape® 2007 A/W Collection/Takarajimasha, Inc.: 122; Hiroki Obara, Courtesy of *Cool Trans*, February 2004: 123; Mari Amita, Courtesy of *Thrill* Magazine, February 2002: 124; P.M. Ken, Courtesy of *Cool Trans*, January 2007: 126; © P.M. Ken, A Bathing Ape® 2006 A/W Collection Ver.1,1 /Takarajimasha, Inc.: 127; Mari Amita, Courtesy of *Ollie* Magazine, August 2005: 128-129; Hiroshi Nomura, Courtesy of *Men's Non-No*/Shueisha, March 2003 (Left-hand Page) & June 2002 (Right-hand Page): 130-131; © Sue Kwon, A Bathing Ape® 2006 S/S Collection Ver.1,1 /Takarajimasha, Inc.: 133; Mari Amita, Courtesy of *Thrill* Magazine, February 2002: 134-135; Mari Amita, Courtesy of *Vita* Magazine, March 2002: 136-137; © Hiroshi Nomura, courtesy of *Smart*/Takarajimasha, Inc., March 2003 (Left-hand Page) & June 2003 (Right-hand Page): 138-139; Yasuyuki Takaki, Courtesy of *Men's Non-No*/Shueisha, 1998: 141; Hidetomo Abe, Courtesy of *Thrill* Magazine, August 2000: 142; © Fumihito Ishii: 143; © Sue Kwon, A Bathing Ape® 2005 S/S Collection Ver.1,1,/ Takarajimasha, Inc.: 144-145; © Mari Amita, A Bathing Ape® 2007 A/W Collection Ver.1,1/ Takarajimasha, Inc.: 146; Hiroshi Nomura, Courtesy of *Men's Non-No*/Shueisha, July 2002: 147; © P. M. Ken, A Bathing Ape® 2007 S/S Collection Ver.1,1/ Takarajimasha, Inc.: 148; © Fumihito Ishii, A Bathing Ape® 2005 A/W Collection Ver.1,1/ Takarajimasha, Inc.: 149; © Shoji Miyake, A Bathing Ape® 2005 A/W Collection Ver.1,1 /Takarajimasha, Inc.: 150; Yasuyuki Takaki, Courtesy of *Men's Non-No*/Shueisha, 1998: 151; Mari Amita, Courtesy of *Ollie* Magazine, January 2004: 152; Hiroshi Nomura, Courtesy of *Men's Non-No*/Shueisha, March 2003: 153; Sue Kwon, Courtesy of *Ollie* Magazine, May 2006: 154; © Shane Nash, Courtesy of *Mass Appeal* Magazine: 155; © Keisuke Naito: 156; © Wing Shya: 157; © Mari Amita, A Bathing Ape® 2005 A/W Collection Ver.1,1/Takarajimasha, Inc.: 158-159; © P.M. Ken, A Bathing Ape® 2007 A/W Collection/Takarajimasha, Inc.: 160; © Mari Amita, *Bessatu Kadokawa* 2006: 161; © Kozo Takayama: 162, 164-165, 166-167; 170-171, 172-173, 174-175; © Masami Sano, Styling by Shino Suganama, A Bathing Ape® 2007 A/W Collection Ver.1,1/Takarajimasha, Inc.: 176-177; © Kozo Takayama: 192-193; © Mari Amita: 202-203; Courtesy of *Weekly Pro-Wresting* Magazine, June 2002: 204, 206-207; © P. M. Ken: 210; Hidetomo Abe for *Asayan*, December 2000: 212; © Yeung Chi Kin Courtesy of *Milk* Magazine, HK October 2007: 216; P. M. Ken: 222; Hiroshi Nomura, © *Weekly Playboy* Magazine/ Shueisha, 13 April 2004: 224, 227; © Getty Images: 231; © Jimmy Cohrssen: 233; Syunya Arai for *Woofin' Girl* Magazine, April 2007/Shinko Music, Styling by Keita Izuka: 242-243; © Tomoki Suzekane, *Men's Non-No* Magazine /Shueisha: 244; © Yasutomo Ebisu, A Bathing Ape® 2005 S/S Collection Ver.1,1/Takarajimasha, Inc.: 245; © Takahito Naito, *LUXG* Magazine /Magazine Box, February 2006: 246; P. M. Ken, A Bathing Ape® 2006 A/W Collection Ver.1,1/ Takarajimasha, Inc.: 248, 250-251; Yasutomo Ebisu for *Huge* No. 4, 2004 © 2008 *Huge* Magazine/Kodansha, Styling by Tsuyoshi Noguchi: 252; © Hiroshi Nomura, courtesy of *Smart*/Takarajimasha, Inc.: 253; Wing Shya, A Bathing Ape® 2006 A/W Collection/Takarajimasha, Inc.: 254-255; Wing Shya for *Asayan*, August 2001: 256-257; Keisuke Naito: 258; © P. M. Ken, A Bathing Ape® 2007 A/W Collection /Takarajimasha, Inc.: 264; © Kozo Takayama: 266; P. M. Ken, A Bathing Ape® 2006 A/W Collection Ver.1,1/Takarajimasha, Inc.: 269; © Kozo Takayama: 270; © *COMPLEX* Magazine, April/May 2006: 273; © Kozo Takayama: 280; Osamu Yokonami for *Spoon* Magazine, Styling by Setsuko Todoroki, April 2004: 282-283; © Hiroshi Nomura, Mini/Takarajimasha, Inc., February 2001: 284-285; Akira Kitajima for *So-En* Magazine/Bunka Publishing, November 2002: 286; Go Relax E More for *Vita* Magazine, Styling: Setsuko Todoroki, April 2002: 287; Kozo Takayama: 288-289; © Toru Furuya for *Numero Tokyo*, November 2006: 290-291; © Keisuke Naito: 292; © Hiroshi Nomura/*Boon* Magazine, January 2001: 298-299; Toru Kogure for *Men's Non-No* Magazine/Shueisha, February 2002, :300-301; Bape Kids® By A Bathing Ape® 2007 A/W Collection/Takarajimasha, Inc.: 304; © P. M. Ken: 305; P. M. Ken for *Relax* Magazine/Magazine House, May 2001: 306; © P. M. Ken: 307; © Hiroshi Nomura/*Boon* Magazine, January 2001: 308; Yoshie Tominaga for *Men's Non-No* Magazine/Shueisha, February 2002, Styling by Tsuyoshi Noguchi: 309; Yoshiaki Tsutsui for *Huge* No. 8, 2004 © 2008 *Huge* Magazine/Kodansha: 311; Katsuya Terada, Courtesy of *Bessatsu Kadokawa*: 312-313; P. M. Ken: 325, 328; © Leslie Kee: 336-339; © Shinichi Sato: 340; © Kozo Takayama: 342-347; © Shinichi Sato: 348; © Kozo Takayama: 349-361; © Junko Yoda: 362-363; © Gregory Goode: 364-365; © Kozo Takayama: 366-367; © Jimmy Cohrssen: 368-373; Karl Lagerfeld, Courtesy of *Interview* Magazine/Bryant Publications: 374; © Jimmy Cohrssen: 378, 383

GATEFOLD LEGEND

PAGE 378:
BAPE STORE® HARAJUKU (2008), DESIGNED WITH **MASAMICHI KATAYA-MA/ WONDERWALL**

PAGE 379-382:
MAGAZINE COVERS FEATURING **A BATHING APE®** AND **NIGO®**

PAGE 383:
BAPE STORE® **LOS ANGELES** (2008), DESIGNED WITH **MASAMICHI KATAYA-MA/ WONDERWALL**

Unless otherwise indicated, images not credited above were provided courtesy of A Bathing Ape.® All product photography not credited above © Yasuhiro Hamasaki.